BALTIMORE UNBOUND

BALTIMORE UNBOUND

Creating
A Greater Baltimore Region
for the
Twenty-first Century

A Strategy Report

by
David Rusk

Published by
The Abell Foundation

The Abell Foundation
111 South Calvert
Suite 2300
Baltimore, MD 21202-6174
Telephone (410) 547-1300

David Rusk/*Baltimore Unbound*

Distributed by
The Johns Hopkins University Press
Hampden Station
Baltimore, Maryland 21211
Order department telephone 1-800-537-5487

Library of Congress Catalog Card Number: 95–79877

ISBN 0–8018–5078–9

TABLE OF CONTENTS

David Rusk is a former mayor of Albuquerque, New Mexico, and a New Mexico state legislator with 30 years experience in urban affairs. He is one of America's foremost champions of regional strategies. His book *Cities Without Suburbs*, originally published in April 1993 by the Woodrow Wilson Center Johns Hopkins University Press, is now in its seventh printing. It combines his political experience and research on population, economic, and social trends for all 522 central cities in the country's 320 metropolitan areas. His findings have seized the interest of public policy makers, academic researchers, and concerned citizens nationwide.

The Abell Foundation
111 S. Calvert Street, Suite 2300 • Baltimore, Maryland 21202

FOREWORD

by Robert C. Embry, Jr., President, The Abell Foundation

When I first read an article by David Rusk on "inelastic cities," I was impressed by his grasp of data concerning regional disparities and failing cities. So much of the discussion prior to Rusk lacked data that demonstrated the decline that many cities face because of uneven regional growth and inflexible political boundaries. I was anxious to find out in more detail about the problems and solutions surrounding Baltimore, given that Rusk had already proclaimed it an inelastic city past the point of no return.

In this publication, Rusk tells the story of a city that he believes is fated to see its problems intensify (dragging the region and state with it) unless there is a dramatic alteration in the balance of wealth and poverty throughout the region. He argues for programs that require that 5 percent of all new housing built in the seven-county region be dedicated to house low-income residents from Baltimore City who elect to move. It is a story that is both troubling and encouraging.

Troubling is the fact that dramatic efforts will be required to balance the regional equation. The source of the leadership required to make the necessary changes is unclear. Also troubling is the possibility that it may again take legal action, as was required to ensure civil rights, to enact a program that provides low-income individuals with opportunities and access to housing in the suburbs. It is troubling that the issue of expanding opportunities for low-income African Americans, especially, is still seen as an arguable proposition when it should be a matter of fact.

But the story presented by Rusk is also encouraging because it is an attempt to get at the root of the problem facing cities: stagnant boundaries and an overwhelmingly disproportionate number of the region's poor people to care for. Promoting a deconcentration of poverty in the city will, in the first instance, provide access to jobs and education for thousands of low-income children and their parents—access they are now denied. Second, it will provide fiscal relief for both city residents and taxpayers alike, in addition to alleviating the social dynamite that is created by concentrated poverty: crime, inadequate education, teenage pregnancy, poor health, and welfare dependency. Deconcentration should also serve to attract a middle class back to the city through the resulting tax relief, an improved quality of life, and better services to those who pay for them.

A recent study by the Federal Reserve Board of Philadelphia concluded that suburbs sink or swim along with their urban center. A drowning city is likely to pull its surrounding region down with it. By making sure that the urban poor are not just reconcentrated in existing, lower-income *suburban* neighborhoods, the recommended program ensures that the problems now facing the city will not be replicated again in, or shifted to, the suburbs. Rusk adds that in Montgomery County, Maryland, neighborhoods that included low-income units in their developments found their resale values to grow faster than their counterparts. A regional housing strategy, properly implemented, appears to be an economic win for all involved.

Most encouraging, however, is the hope that a regional housing strategy will open up opportunities for poor people to succeed in the suburbs, which has been successfully demonstrated in Chicago through the Gautreaux Housing Initiative. In Chicago, public housing residents who elected to move to suburbs under a court-induced program fared far better than their counterparts who did not move in high school graduation rates, college entrance, and employment. As many others have already found, the suburbs can be a truly uplifting experience for all. People who choose to live in the suburbs should be provided an opportunity to do so.

Though Baltimore, like many older communities, takes slowly to change, there is much precedent for it in the region's history. The pattern appears to be indelible: at first, there is resistance; then resistance becomes acceptance; and very soon the change that was once feared is embraced as invaluable to the community's well-being. Some examples of this cycle have appeared in the Baltimore *Evening Sun* as "Baltimore Glimpses." With permission, we include a selected few throughout the text to make the point.

The Rusk report makes bold recommendations that deserve discussion and, if found to be valid, action. On behalf of The Abell Foundation, I am pleased to offer this report as a contribution to what needs to be an ongoing debate about the issue.

AUTHOR'S PREFACE

There may be those—black and white—who take offense at the racial focus of this report's analysis and characterizations, but reversing Baltimore City's constant decline must begin with frank discussion of poverty *and* race. Being poor and black isn't just an "economic problem," as many would have us believe. Poor urban blacks drop out of school more, have fewer jobs, draw more welfare, have more illegitimate babies, use more drugs, commit more crimes, and murder each other more than do poor urban whites.

This social meltdown is the result of poor blacks being packed into ghetto neighborhoods, increasingly isolated from the rest of Baltimore society. We cannot even compare crime rates, addiction rates, or illegitimacy rates among poor blacks and poor whites in comparable circumstances *because almost nowhere in the Baltimore area are poor whites as ghettoized as poor blacks.* There are almost no comparable circumstances.

This report is not an exercise in fixing blame. The growing racial and economic isolation of Baltimore City—at least as a place for middle class families to live—reflects patterns of suburbanization and central city decline that are common to many American communities. In part, the severe economic ghettoization of poor blacks today is an unintended consequence of the success of the civil rights movement. Today, half of the Baltimore area's upper middle class black households live in suburbia. Fewer than one out of five continues to live in city areas with significant numbers of poor black neighbors. In some measure the growing isolation of poor blacks reflects choices made by middle class blacks.

I do not fault such choices. A middle class black family has no special responsibility to endure living in a deteriorating neighborhood, beset by high crime rates, poor public services, and bad schools. I believe that all heads of households—white or black—have the right to seek the best homes, safest neighborhoods, and best schools for their families.

The problem is that the Baltimore community does not offer any reasonable range of housing and neighborhood choices for poor black households. (Poor white households are scattered much more widely around the metro area). Creating that choice is the heart of this report's recommendations. The experience of some other urban areas is that, faced with real choice in housing and neighborhoods, most poor black families will indeed choose the better opportunities.

This report may be charged with racial paternalism (particularly as the product of a white author). Under many different guises, "community empowerment" is a perennial and popular theme of social reformers. Why not through community development banks . . . neighborhood development corporations . . . nonprofit housing programs . . . enterprise zones . . . job training programs, etc. just help poor people better their circumstances where they are?

As a veteran of running such programs, I understand the valuable appeal to personal and community pride—indeed, to racial pride—that such programs make. Yet the crux of the issue is simply *where have they worked*? There are no cities in this country whose decline has been reversed by such programs. Despite short-term successes, there are few neighborhoods that have been stabilized over the long term. "Such programs," a former (black) mayor of Saginaw, Michigan, once said to me, "expect the poor to save the poor."

The situation is akin to a crowd of people trying to run up the down escalator. No matter how hard they run, the escalator comes back down faster. Most social programs try to help poor people run up faster. The ablest and most determined may compete so well (or some programs may be so effective) that a few may successfully reach the top of the down escalator and jump off. But the rest—along with their neighbors—are carried back downward to the bottom.

The recommendations of this report would rewire that escalator so that it carries poor blacks upward (and outward)—an escalator that flows *with* rather than *against* community-based social programs.

The hyperconcentration of black poverty within Baltimore City neighborhoods is not just "the black community's problem" to solve. In one way or another, all have contributed to it, and all are victimized by it. It is everybody's problem to solve.

DAVID RUSK

David Rusk is a former mayor of Albuquerque (1977–81), and New Mexico state legislator (1975–77). He has over 30 years of experience in urban affairs.

His first book, *Cities Without Suburbs* (Woodrow Wilson Center and Johns Hopkins University Press: April 1993), is now in its sixth printing. It combines his political experiences with his research on population, economic, and social trends for all 522 central cities in the country's 320 metropolitan areas. He wrote the book as Guest Scholar on Urban Affairs for the Woodrow Wilson International Center for Scholars.

Cities Without Suburbs has proposed "a genuinely revolutionary idea," said Mickey Kaus (*The New Republic*). John Gallagher (*Detroit Free Press*) concluded that "every mayor, every governor, every country executive, indeed anyone who cares about our great but ailing cities ought to read it."

Rusk is an independent consultant on urban and suburban policy now based in Washington, D.C. Since the publication of *Cities Without Suburbs* he has traveled to over 60 U.S. communities, speaking to local governments, business groups, national associations, regional organizations, and academic forums. In 1994 he lectured on urban problems in Berlin, Stuttgart, and Frankfurt, Germany for the U.S. State Department. He has been lead witness before legislative bodies in Connecticut, Virginia, and Minnesota. Mr. Rusk also writes extensively, publishing articles in *The New York Times, Newsday* and *State Government News,* among others. He has collaborated with local newspapers in over 90 communities.

Mr. Rusk graduated from the University of California at Berkeley in 1962. From 1963–68 he was a full-time civil rights and anti-poverty worker with the Washington Urban League. He then entered the U.S. Department of Labor, serving as the Manpower Administration's legislative and program director.

BALTIMORE UNBOUND
EXECUTIVE SUMMARY

What is the future of the Baltimore region? Will a resurgent Baltimore City prosper as the employment, cultural, and civic heart of urban Maryland—a great place to work, to visit, *and* to live? Or will a slowly foundering Baltimore City become a second Detroit—a once great metropolis now treated as a giant public housing project—and pull the whole Baltimore region down with it?

This is the choice that the governor and the Maryland General Assembly face. The city and the state have carried out exemplary (if traditional) revitalization efforts. Unfortunately, Charles Center, the Inner Harbor, Oriole Park at Camden Yards, and the hundreds of millions of dollars of state subsidies have only slowed but not reversed Baltimore City's steady erosion as a place to live.

THE NECESSITY

Quite simply, Baltimore City is programmed for inexorable decline. Like so many "inelastic" cities, Baltimore City is prevented from growing along with its metropolitan region. During four decades of constant urbanization, the Baltimore region has expanded from three counties to seven counties, but "inelastic" Baltimore City has been locked within its 80.8 square miles since 1918. While the Baltimore region added 910,000 new residents from 1950 to 1990, Baltimore City lost 182,000 residents. In 1950, the average city family earned 92 percent of the average suburban family's income; by 1990, city family incomes had slid to only 59 percent of suburban levels. Although the civil rights revolution has opened up suburban neighborhoods, most black suburbanites are overwhelmingly middle class. The result is that poor blacks are increasingly isolated within older Baltimore City neighborhoods.

As a community to live in, Baltimore City is programmed to decline because it must house a disproportionate share of the region's poor blacks. Within the region, Baltimore City contains more than twice its proportionate share of the urban poor of all races and 86 percent of all poor blacks. Almost half of city neighborhoods are "poverty neighborhoods" where 20 percent or more of the residents fall below the poverty line. In one-fifth of city neighborhoods, more than 40 percent of the residents are poor.

Of the region's 137,000 poor blacks, almost three-quarters (72 percent) live in poor neighborhoods—almost 32 percent live in neighborhoods of extreme poverty. By contrast, of the region's 90,000 poor whites, only one in four (24 percent) live in poor neighborhoods.

Such hyperconcentration of minority poor creates social dynamite—high crime rates, drug addiction, family disintegration, welfare dependency, and illegitimacy. Caught between rising service needs and a relatively shrinking tax base, Baltimore City government is in a constant fiscal squeeze. Social dynamite and fiscal crisis are the topic of daily headlines and TV news reports. It is not the role of this study to document the well-known catalog of problems once again but to emphasize that inner-city social chaos is the inescapable result of patterns of metropolitan development the Baltimore area shares with many other metro areas.

There is a "point of no return" for cities—a combination of high population loss, disproportionately high minority population, and great disparities between city and suburban income levels. There are 34 American cities, including, by 1980, Baltimore City, that have passed the point of no return. *Not one of these cities has subsequently ever closed the income gap with its suburbs by so much as one percentage point!* No combination of urban renewal, downtown development, model cities programs, community development corporations and, I predict, enterprise or empowerment zones has ever reversed the downward slide of such cities. There is no factual basis for believing that more of the same, including Baltimore City's new federally funded empowerment zone, will reverse Baltimore City's decline—and Baltimore City has been one of the ablest practitioners of such programs.

To be beyond the point of no return is not cause for abandoning all hope. Progress, however, requires recognizing and acting on the core problem: the city's growing social and economic isolation. As places to live, such cities are slowly being abandoned to the black poor, who are themselves the primary victims of such abandonment. To end growing isolation requires conscious, purposeful public policies either to enlarge the city geographically (hence socially and economically as well) or to end the city's role as poorhouse for the region's minority poor.

THE ALTERNATIVES

No community is exempt from America's social ills, but there are hundreds of more "elastic" cities that have largely avoided similar social and economic isolation within their metropolitan regions. They have the legal authority to expand their boundaries as their regions grow. Many cities such as Houston, Charlotte, and Columbus have expanded through aggressive annexation of urbanizing areas. A few cities such as Indianapolis, Nashville, and Jacksonville have consolidated city and county governments. Both methods enlarge cities geographically to incorporate large areas of their "suburbs" within their own city boundaries.

It is too late to enlarge Baltimore City geographically. A state constitutional amendment adopted in 1948 prevents Baltimore City from further annexations or (probably) from city-county consolidation without approval of suburban voters. That approval would never be given. Moreover, expanding Baltimore City by annexing, for example, all of Baltimore County inside the Beltway would not change Baltimore City's character as a poorer, blacker enclave at the region's core. Consolidating Baltimore City and all of Baltimore County would have a much greater positive impact; however, city-county consolidation would not open up access to the metro area's most rapidly growing neighborhoods, particularly in Howard and Anne Arundel Counties.

What must be done is to relieve Baltimore City of its role as the region's poorhouse. The mayor and council of Baltimore City cannot accomplish this by themselves. They have neither the financial tools nor the legal authority to end Baltimore City's isolation among its neighbors. Nor is it likely that cooperative intergovernmental agreements could be reached voluntarily among city and suburban officials. At the center of the "urban problem" are the toughest political issues in American society—poverty *and* race. Local officials may be willing to "take care of our own poor" (sometimes in very enlightened ways, as in nearby Montgomery County). Local officials never voluntarily agree to take care of their neighbors' poor.

State government must take the lead. State government determines how local governments are organized and what their responsibilities are. The state legislature and the governor must act as a metro-wide policy body. They must, in effect, reprogram how the Baltimore region works to reverse Baltimore City's social and economic isolation. The key is to require the entire metro region to become home of the metro area's poor on a "fair share" basis.

Sharing the burden of poverty is a more daunting political task than it is a heavy social or economic burden. Of every 100 residents of the Baltimore region, fewer than four are both poor and white (and three out of four poor whites are already living in middle class neighborhoods, mostly in the suburbs). And of every 100 residents of the Baltimore region fewer than six are both poor and black (but almost three out of four poor blacks live in poor inner-city neighborhoods). In 1990, the 2.4 million residents of the Baltimore region earned $32 billion of annual income and owned most of the area's $100 billion in commercial, industrial, and residential property. Unlike many Third World societies, the Baltimore region is not overwhelmed by hordes of poor people. In the Baltimore region the poor are few, the middle class are many. The problem is not the overall level of poverty. The problem is the high concentration of poverty among black residents in many Baltimore City neighborhoods.

The Baltimore region as a whole has the social and economic capacity to absorb the minority poor into middle class neighborhoods readily if it has the will to do so. That political will must be supplied through the political processes of state government.

THE STRATEGY

To reprogram how the Baltimore region functions, the Maryland General Assembly should enact a state statute to create a Municipality of Metropolitan Baltimore, or "Metro" (following legislatures' precedents for Portland, Oregon and Toronto, Ontario). Metro's jurisdiction would cover Baltimore City and the six counties that currently comprise the Baltimore Metropolitan Statistical Area (Baltimore County and Anne Arundel, Carroll, Harford, Howard, and Queen Anne's Counties).

Metro would function as the upper tier of a two-tier system of local government. No existing local government would be abolished. However, Metro's central mission would be to carry out the metro-wide planning, zoning, and housing assistance programs that are necessary to dissolve the high concentration of poverty in many Baltimore City neighborhoods. At the same time, Metro would protect suburban neighborhoods from becoming the next generation's slums, as is now occurring in so many older, inner suburbs around the country. "Diversity, balance, stability" would be Metro's themes.

Metro would be governed by a Metropolitan Council, directly elected to represent the seven districts into which the metro area would be divided (again, examples are Portland and Toronto). It would be headed by a directly elected Metro Executive (Portland).

Metro would be endowed by the General Assembly with the general powers of any other municipality (and of any county to the extent that counties have powers that are not available to municipalities). However, Metro would carry out only policy functions and public services assigned it by the General Assembly, requested by local governments, or approved by vote of its constituents (as in Portland).

Metro's purpose would not be to provide general governmental services but, as stated in its central mission, to redirect patterns of urban development that are now fostering growing social inequities by race and income class. Its key responsibilities and powers (as authorized by the General Assembly) would include

1. enacting a metro-wide "fair share" low- and moderate-income housing ordinance (as Montgomery County has had in operation for 23 years) and monitoring local governments' adherence to its provisions;
2. establishing a Metro-operated "Housing Opportunities Commission," which would
   a. absorb the assets, operations, and responsibilities of the various public housing agencies maintained by constituent governments to manage a regionwide public housing program (like Metro Toronto);
   b. take over the housing finance functions of housing finance agencies of local governments or the State of Maryland for the metro area; and
   c. establish a range of rental assistance and purchase programs for low- and moderate-income households throughout the Baltimore region similar to the array of programs operated by Montgomery County.

To provide the comprehensive development policy framework for its housing programs, the state-authorized powers for Metro would also include

3. establishing a regionwide comprehensive land use plan in conjunction with local governments (Portland, Toronto, Seattle);
4. designating an urban growth boundary (Portland, Seattle) and establishing adequate public facilities requirements (Montgomery County, Toronto) to bring about rational growth management and to balance housing production with demand throughout the region;

5. monitoring adherence of local plans, infrastructure investments, and zoning actions with the adopted general plan (Portland, Toronto, Seattle);

6. serving as the Metropolitan Planning Organization for transportation planning within the region, including the allocation of federal funds under the Intermodal Surface Transportation Efficiency Act (Portland); and

7. establishing a regionwide revenue sharing program (Metro Tax Base Pool) by pooling a portion of property tax base growth from new commercial, industrial, and high-end residential property throughout the region (Twin Cities).

Metro's core administrative costs would be supported by a small uniform property tax millage levied against all residential, commercial, and industrial property throughout its jurisdiction. This millage rate, including any maximum ceiling, would be set forth in the authorizing legislation by the General Assembly (Portland).

Metro's housing programs would be supported by the combination of federal and state grants that currently fund such programs plus use of whatever portion of the Metro Tax Base Pool the Metro Council decides is necessary to achieve its low-income housing goals. For any other nonhousing activity, Metro could levy taxes for its operating budget and capital requirements only as authorized by the General Assembly, participating local governments, or a majority of voters of its jurisdiction.

A. The "Fair Share" Housing Program

As authorized by state law, Metro's "fair share" housing program would be patterned on Montgomery County's highly successful Moderately-Priced Dwelling Unit (MPDU) policy. Metro's housing policy would require that, for every housing development of 50 or more units, the developer would have to sell or rent 10 percent of the units to moderate-income households and sell another 5 percent of the units directly to Metro's Housing Opportunities Commission (HOC) as scattered site public housing. (The developer would be compensated for potential loss from selling or renting 15 percent of the units at below market prices by receiving a "density bonus" allowing construction of up to 22 percent more units than allowable by normal zoning standards.)

If, in the seven-county region, 20,000 new housing units are built each year for the next 20 years, Metro's HOC would acquire about 500 newly constructed units each year scattered throughout the metro area. Most would be in the most rapidly developing new areas. At current prices, it would cost about $50–60 million a year to acquire the units. Metro's HOC would never build "public housing projects." It would simply buy or rent standard housing on a highly scattered basis for deep-subsidy households.

If each suburban county's fair share of poor households were set, for example, at 6.5 percent of its total population, over the next 20 years Harford, Howard, and Queen Anne's Counties would meet their fair share goals entirely through the HOC's purchase of its 5 percent share of new construction in those counties. Anne Arundel, Carroll, and Baltimore Counties would meet at least two-thirds of their goals through the HOC's share of new construction.

To fulfill the remaining need, the Metro HOC would have to purchase or rent existing housing in existing neighborhoods. Great care would be taken not to affect any existing suburban neighborhoods adversely by acquiring too much housing for low-income households. Saving city poverty neighborhoods by creating new slums in the suburbs makes no sense. By focusing on new construction, the 5 percent set-aside for the HOC's direct purchase is both a minimum *and a maximum* for low-income households in *new* neighborhoods.

After 20 years the net effect of such policies would be that each suburban county's population would have 6.5 percent poor households compared with a current range of 2.2 percent (Howard County) to 4.9 percent (Carroll County), yet this would still be less than the projected regional average of 8 percent. The proportion of poor black households would range from 3.0 percent (Baltimore County) to 4.6 percent (Howard County). Meanwhile, the level of poverty in Baltimore City overall would have been cut in half, and poor black residents would be just 7.1 percent of all city households. Overall, the level of poverty within the region would probably drop from 10 percent to about 8 percent simply by moving poor households out of inner-city neighborhoods that offer little opportunity into suburban areas that offer better educational and employment opportunities.

B. The Metro Tax Base Pool

Under another state law, Metro would institute a tax base sharing program like the Twin Cities Fiscal Disparities Plan that has been in operation since 1975 for the seven-county, 188-municipality Minneapolis–St. Paul area. From the inception of the Metro tax base sharing program, 40 percent of the *increase* in assessed value of commercial, industrial, and high-end residential property (i.e., homes at 150 percent of the metro area's median home value) would be allocated to the Metro Tax Base Pool. Local governments would keep 60 percent of the increased value and would retain full control over all past property valuation (i.e., the level prior to the initial year of the tax base sharing program).

The Metro Council would set the tax rate for the Metro Tax Base Pool and control its allocation. For example, the Metro Council might set the uniform rate on pooled property at 4 percent of assessed value. This would be well below Baltimore City's current rate (5.95 percent) but above current suburban county rates (2.35–2.90 percent). If we anticipate a 5 percent annual increase in assessed valuation, this would yield about $19–20 million in revenues the first year. Actual revenues collected would increase steadily as the Metro Tax Base Pool expanded with each year's annual growth increment. By the twentieth year, the pool's revenues would exceed $600 million per year.

For the first three years, the Metro Council should allocate all the pool's revenues to its own housing programs. By the third year, however, the pool's growth would exceed Metro's housing needs (i.e., $50–60 million per year). It could then begin to share revenues back with local jurisdictions.

The small property tax increase proposed would represent less than two-tenths of 1 percent of personal income for all the region's residents. For this monetary sacrifice, the people of the Baltimore region could substantially end the high concentration of poor people in Baltimore City neighborhoods and arrest the spread of poverty to older suburbs of Baltimore County and Anne Arundel County. By ending the high concentration of poverty, regional crime rates would fall, unemployment would drop, welfare rolls would shrink, and school achievement levels would rise. Over time, with crime and welfare falling, state taxes might fall as well. The key is to have the right policy and to apply that policy in a sustained, consistent manner over 15–20 years.

• • •

What the Baltimore region currently needs most is neither the example of a successful plan (which Montgomery County offers) nor more money (the region can afford the cost of corrective action itself). What the Baltimore region needs is a political breakthrough. That breakthrough must come from Maryland's governor and legislature.

The policies recommended here are neither politically painless nor politically easy. Poverty and race combine to create the toughest political issue in America. The Baltimore region stands on the threshold of the 21st century. Today, Baltimore City—Maryland's signature city—is gripped relentlessly by a process of slow economic and social decline. The State of Maryland must summon the political will and the political courage to recapture for Baltimore City that front rank among American communities it once proudly held. And with the renewed health of Baltimore City comes the best assurance of sustained, vigorous economic growth for the whole Baltimore region.

Introduction

The 1990 census gives the Baltimore area much cause for self-congratulation.

- According to the 1990 census, metro Baltimore is the 20th wealthiest metropolitan area in the United States and has had the 16th fastest rate of increase in per capita income over the past two decades;
- The Baltimore area is increasingly integrated economically with the Washington, D.C. metropolitan area, the nation's wealthiest and 13th fastest growing economically; and
- The level of poverty in the Baltimore area has declined from 12 percent to 10 percent (1969–1989).

Beyond cold census data, Baltimoreans can also take pride in the observations that

- The metropolitan area has made a successful transition from a manufacturing-based to a services-based economy over the last 40 years;
- Downtown Baltimore continues to be the employment, civic, cultural, and recreational focal point of the metropolitan region through the Charles Center, the Inner Harbor, Camden Yards, and other redevelopment projects that have been executed with a style, taste, and scope unsurpassed among American cities; and
- Baltimore City has had excellent political leadership for almost 25 years under Mayor William Donald Schaefer and Mayor Kurt Schmoke.

However, the growth and prosperity of the Baltimore region are imperiled by the steady decline of Baltimore City as a place to live. The social deterioration of most city neighborhoods erodes Baltimore City's vitality and threatens its attractiveness not only as a place to live but as a place to work, to shop, and to visit.

Over the last four decades (1950–1990), Baltimore City has:

- lost 23 percent of its population;
- shrunk in regional importance, dropping from 71 percent to 31 percent of its metropolitan population;
- seen the average income of city families drop from 92 percent to 59 percent of the average income of suburban families;
- had the black population of Baltimore City increase to a disproportionate 60 percent through white flight from the city; and
- experienced chronic fiscal crisis in city government.

The heart of Baltimore City's slow decline is that it is cast in a highly specialized role within the metropolitan community: Baltimore City must house, educate, and serve the social service needs of far too many poor black residents. Baltimore City has over two times its "fair share" of the poor black population of its metropolitan area.

According to the precedent of other cities on—but farther down—the same path of decline, Baltimore City will continue to weaken. Its social and economic erosion will be measured by:

- the growing concentration of the metropolitan area's poor black population within Baltimore City;
- the continued flight of middle class families (white and black) from both the Baltimore public schools and Baltimore City's neighborhoods;
- the continued spread of deteriorating, poverty-impacted neighborhoods across the city's face;
- the shriveling up of retail activity in the city as city residents' buying power shrinks and suburban consumers shun traditional city retailers because of the fear—and reality—of crime;
- the gradual inability of downtown Baltimore to compete for and retain office locations of blue-chip employers;
- the growing inability of poor city residents to get jobs in the growing metropolitan economy because of skill and transportation barriers;
- a growing incidence of crime, drug and alcohol abuse, illegitimacy, and welfare dependency among city residents;
- a widening gap between city government revenues and expenditures for both basic municipal functions and poverty-targeted social services due to the expansion and growth of highly segregated, poor neighborhoods;

- increased Baltimore City reliance on city and federal aid; and
- further deterioration of the city government's creditworthiness and increased cost of governmental borrowing.

The consequences of Baltimore City's unchecked decline for the Baltimore region and the state of Maryland will be:

- retarded economic growth for the whole region, particularly for the northern counties (Baltimore, Harford, and Carroll) without Baltimore City as a strong employment center;
- the gradual deterioration of Baltimore County as Baltimore City's social blight extends into older suburban neighborhoods in Baltimore County;
- the growing dominance of Anne Arundel and Howard Counties' economic ties to the Washington, D.C. metropolitan area;
- increased demands on state government to transfer wealth from Washington's Maryland suburbs to Baltimore City and its distressed suburbs;
- loss of Baltimore City as Maryland's historic and traditional urban center, defining Maryland's urban character; and
- in effect, conversion of the State of Maryland into a Maryland division of the Washington metro area.

Baltimore City's steady erosion is inevitable unless radical action is taken. The goal of such action must be to relieve Baltimore City of its specialized role as the warehouse of most of the metro area's poor blacks. This must be accomplished either

1. by redefining Baltimore City as a larger share of the growing metropolitan area, expanding the city's social, economic, and fiscal base, or
2. by establishing new, metropolitan-wide requirements for all local jurisdictions to accept "fair shares" of the area's poor blacks and to tax the wealth of the whole region more equitably to support the necessary public services.

Either course of reform will require courageous, bold, and resolute action by Maryland's governor and General Assembly. Such reforms are beyond the constitutional authority and political capabilities of local elected officials.

This report will make a compelling argument why action *must* be taken and will present a detailed blueprint for the necessary reforms to do so.

Chapter One, "The Necessity," will demonstrate how, unless there is radical change, Baltimore City is on the path of constant decline that has been followed by similar cities. It will also contrast Baltimore's fate with the fate of other cities that, despite basic population similarities with the Baltimore region, follow a different path—and with different, more successful outcomes.

Chapter Two, "The Alternatives," will examine successful specific strategies that have been used in other metropolitan areas for avoiding the severe racial and economic isolation that is Baltimore City's burden and the region's peril.

Chapter Three, "The Strategy," will set forth specific proposals for reforms that must be carried out throughout the greater Baltimore region to restore Baltimore City as the viable urban center of the state of Maryland.

BALTIMORE UNBOUND

CHAPTER ONE

THE NECESSITY

Baltimore City's economic and social decline is not unique. It is caused by patterns of growth that are common to about 40 percent of America's 320 metro areas.

Over the last four decades, urban America has undergone a profound transformation. In 1950, almost 60 percent of the population of America's 168 metro areas lived in 193 central cities. Ten of America's 12 largest cities, including Baltimore City, hit their population peaks in the 1950 census.

By 1990, even though the population of America's now 320 designated metropolitan areas had doubled, over 60 percent of the metro population lived in suburbs outside central cities. In effect, all net population growth was low-density, suburban-style growth. Even inside central cities, population density had thinned out. Between 1950 and 1990, the density of population of America's 522 central cities dropped by one-half—from 5,873 people per square mile in 1950 to 2,937 people per square mile in 1990.[1]

What happened to central cities depended on how they adjusted to this era of universal suburban-style growth. "Elastic cities" either had a large inventory of undeveloped land within their municipal boundaries or were able to expand their municipal area through annexation or, more rarely, through consolidation with their surrounding counties.[2] Elastic cities captured a substantial share of suburban-style growth within their own city limits.

For a variety of historical, legal, and political reasons, by 1950, many "inelastic cities" were already trapped within existing municipal limits. After some initial expansion, others ceased to expand territorially by about 1970. Inelastic cities failed to capture suburban-style growth. Typically, they also lost population, contributing substantially to their own suburbs' population growth.

---

[1] For the 193 central cities identified as such in the 1950 census, the average density in 1950 was 7,517 people per square mile.

[2] See the author's *Cities without Suburbs*. The Woodrow Wilson Center Press/Johns Hopkins University Press. Washington, DC-Baltimore, MD (April 1993).

For both central cities and their suburbs, the economic, social, and fiscal consequences have been profound. Why cities were elastic or inelastic and the resulting consequences are analyzed in this chapter.

SELECTING BALTIMORE'S PEERS

To place the Baltimore region in context, 21 other metropolitan areas have been identified that were similar to the Baltimore region in 1950. The 21 metro areas, plus the Baltimore region, are shown in Table 1.1. First, all these metro areas had roughly the same racial composition in 1950 as metro Baltimore. In 1950, metro Baltimore had a black population of 20 percent. The other 21 metro areas fell within a range of not less than 50 percent below nor more than 50 percent above the proportion of black

TABLE 1.1
22 metro areas by population size and % black in 1950
(population in 1,000s)

Metropolitan Area	Metro Population, 1950[1]	Metro % Black, 1950
St. Louis, MO	1,807	12%
Washington, DC	1,639	23%
Cleveland, OH	1,533	11%
Newark, NJ	1,503	12%
Baltimore, MD	**1,472**	**20%**
Oakland, CA	1,039	11%
Cincinnati, OH	1,023	11%
Kansas City, MO	952	11%
Atlanta, GA	936	25%
Houston, TX	901	19%
Dallas, TX	781	14%
New Orleans, LA	741	29%
Columbus, OH	729	10%
Indianapolis, IN	727	12%
Louisville, KY-IN	635	12%
Charlotte, NC	588	25%
Greensboro, NC	509	23%
Nashville, TN	502	20%
Richmond, VA	463	27%
Norfolk, VA	395	28%
Jacksonville, FL	356	27%
Raleigh, NC	304	30%

[1]For this study, metro areas in 1950 are comprised of the same county jurisdictions they have in 1990.

population in metro Baltimore. The percentages ranged from a low of 10 percent (Columbus, Ohio) to a high of 30 percent (Raleigh-Durham). In terms of other minorities, all had minimal Hispanic, Asian, and Native American populations.

Second, 13 of these metro areas fell within a population range not less than 50 percent below nor more than 50 percent above metro Baltimore's 1950 population (1.472 million.) Metro areas that were substantially larger (New York, Chicago, Los Angeles, Philadelphia, and Detroit) were eliminated.

Finally, included in the analysis are eight metro areas that approximated the Baltimore area's racial profile but had less than 50 percent of metro Baltimore's population in 1950. These eight— Louisville, Norfolk, Richmond, Charlotte, Nashville, Jacksonville, Raleigh-Durham, and Greensboro–Winson-Salem–High Point— are all located within 500 miles of Baltimore and by 1990 had become regional competitors. More significant for this analysis, they all exhibit varying growth characteristics that illustrate the importance of urban elasticity.

CALCULATING A CITY'S ELASTICITY

Two factors—initial population density and rate of expansion of municipal territory—combine to define a city's elasticity. Table 1.2 examines each city's population density in 1950 and the degree to which each city expanded its municipal territory between 1950 and 1990.

City population densities in 1950 ranged from a low of 2,861 people per square mile (New Orleans) to a high of 18,592 people per square mile (Newark). New Orleans' low figure is suspect, however, since much of New Orleans' municipal area embraces difficult-to-develop Mississippi River delta acreage. In reality, only Dallas (66 percent), Houston (63 percent), Charlotte (76 percent), and Greensboro (70 percent) fell significantly below the average national density for central cities. These cities had some modest room to absorb population growth within existing city limits.

All other cities had to expand in area to grow in population without increasing density. Indeed, with falling household sizes, all needed to expand in size even to retain their 1950 population levels over the next 40 years.

At 12,067 inhabitants per square mile (205 percent or twice the national average), Baltimore City clearly had to acquire new land even to maintain its 1950 population level.

Typically, the densely populated cities that needed to expand most expanded least or not at all. Washington, D.C.'s maximum

TABLE 1.2
Elasticity scores by category for 22 metro areas

City by Elasticity Category	City Density, 1950	% National Density Average	City Area 1950 (sq. mi.)	City Area 1990 (sq. mi.)	City Area Growth	City Elasticity Score
Zero						
Washington, DC	13,065	222%	61	61	0%	4
Cleveland, OH	12,197	208%	75	77	3%	4
Newark, NJ	18,592	317%	24	24	1%	4
St. Louis, MO	14,046	239%	61	62	1%	4
Baltimore, MD	**12,067**	**205%**	**79**	**81**	**3%**	**4**
Oakland, CA	7,256	124%	53	56	6%	6
Cincinnati, OH	6,711	114%	75	77	3%	7
Zero, mean	**11,991**	**204%**	**61**	**63**	**3%**	
Low-Medium						
New Orleans, LA	2,861	49%	199	181	–9%	12
Louisville, KY	9,251	158%	40	62	56%	14
Norfolk, VA	7,571	129%	28	54	91%	15
Richmond, VA	6,208	106%	37	60	62%	17
Atlanta, GA	8,979	153%	37	132	257%	23
Columbus, OH	9,541	162%	39	191	385%	26
Kansas City, MO	5,665	96%	81	312	322%	26
Dallas, TX	3,879	66%	112	342	206%	26
Low-medium, mean	**6,744**	**115%**	**72**	**167**	**132%**	
High-Hyper						
Houston, TX	3,726	63%	160	540	237%	29
Charlotte, NC	4,468	76%	30	174	481%	30
Indianapolis, IN	7,739	132%	55	362	555%	30
Raleigh, NC	5,971	102%	11	88	550%	32
Greensboro, NC	4,087	70%	18	80	314%	32
Nashville, TN	7,923	135%	22	473	2,051%	33
Jacksonville, FL	6,772	115%	30	759	2,412%	34
High-hyper, mean	**5,812**	**99%**	**47**	**354**	**653%**	

boundaries are fixed by the federal Constitution. The minimal territorial expansion recorded for Cleveland, Newark, St. Louis, Baltimore, Oakland, and Cincinnati was probably the result of more accurate surveying and of reclaiming riverfront and lakefront land. (New Orleans may have lost "land" to redefinition of jurisdiction over waterways.) Louisville, Norfolk, Richmond, Kansas City, and Atlanta all annexed new lands during the 1950s and 1960s, then were halted in their expansion. Columbus, Dallas, Houston, Charlotte, Raleigh, and Greensboro annexed aggressively throughout the period. By consolidating with their surrounding counties, Indianapolis, Nashville, and Jacksonville were the champion expansionists of the 22 cities.

These two factors—initial population density and rate of municipal area expansion—combine to define a city's elasticity.

To rank cities by their elasticities, 117 principal central cities in metro areas of 200,000 or more residents are compared. Cities are first ranked by 1950 population density into deciles. Cities with the highest densities are in the first decile; those with the lowest densities are in the tenth decile. In similar fashion, cities are ranked into deciles by percentage increase in their municipal area. Cities with no or little increase are in the first decile; those with the highest increase are in the tenth decile.

Acquiring new territory has about three times the impact on a city's ability to obtain new population growth as having had an inventory of undeveloped land within existing city limits in 1950.[3] Therefore, to calculate the combined effect, or a city's elasticity score, a city's initial density ranking and three times its area expansion ranking are added together.

According to these calculations, Baltimore City ranks in the worst deciles (first) in terms of both initial density and area expansion. Its elasticity score is 4, that is, $1 + (3 \times 1) = 4$. By contrast, Jacksonville ranks in the fourth decile in initial density but, through city-county consolidation, is in the best, or tenth, decile in area expansion. Its elasticity score is 34, that is, $4 + (3 \times 10) = 34$.

The 22 cities are grouped by elasticity score in Table 1.2 into categories of "zero elasticity," "low-medium elasticity," and "high-hyper elasticity." Because the number of areas studied in this report is relatively small, I have combined categories that would otherwise clearly stand apart as in *Cities without Suburbs*, in which 117 of the largest metro areas are analyzed.

Table 1.2 shows the striking differences in density and expansion among the three groups. In 1950, the seven zero elasticity cities had twice the average density of development (11,991 people per square mile, or an index of 204 percent of the national average). Over the next 40 years, they hardly expanded at all in municipal territory (from an average of 61 to 63 square miles, or just 3 percent). The eight low-medium elasticity cities were generally above the national density average in 1950 (6,744 or an index of 115 percent). However, they expanded substantially (from an average of 72 square miles to 167 square miles, or 132 percent). Finally, the seven high-hyper density cities hit right on the national

---

[3]The original elasticity index in *Cities without Suburbs* gave equal weight to initial population density and rate of area expansion.

average city density in 1950 (5,812, or an index of 99 percent); however, they all expanded dramatically (from an average of 47 square miles to 354 square miles, or 653 percent).

In 1950, all central cities fell within roughly the same range in area (from 11 square miles to 75 square miles) except Dallas, Houston, and New Orleans. Over the next 40 years, the medium-, high-, and hyper-elastic cities grew much larger, with Nashville (473 sq. mi.), Houston (540 sq. mi.), and Jacksonville (759 sq. mi.) each approaching the geographic area of Baltimore City (81 sq. mi.) and Baltimore County (599 sq. mi.) *combined.*

From this point forward in the analysis, statistical results will be summarized by each of the three elasticity groups (zero, low-medium, and high-hyper), setting out the specific results for Baltimore within the zero elasticity category.

GROWING CITIES, SHRINKING CITIES

From 1950 onward, all 22 metropolitan areas grew in population (Table 1.3). The rates of growth were generally greatest for the metro areas that began with smaller population bases. As a group, the high-hyper category began with an average metro population of 555,000 in 1950. High-hyper metro areas more than doubled their population (131 percent growth) over the next 40 years. However, though their rates of growth were lower (60 percent), the zero elasticity category added an average of 846,000 new residents—lower absolute growth than the low-medium group (894,000) but higher than the high-hyper group (771,000). With 910,000 new residents, the Baltimore region ranked seventh out of 22 in absolute population growth.

TABLE 1.3
Population growth of 22 metro areas summarized by
elasticity groupings and compared to metro Baltimore
(Population in 1,000s)

Classification	Metro Population, 1950	Metro Population, 1990	Metro Population Change	Metro Population % Growth
Zero elasticity	1,431	2,277	846	60%
Baltimore Metro	**1,472**	**2,382**	**910**	**62%**
Low-medium elasticity	704	1,598	894	127%
High-hyper elasticity	555	1,326	771	131%

By contrast, population trends in the central cities were radically different (Table 1.4). Between 1950 and 1990, the high-hyper elasticity cities more than doubled in population (155 percent), growing from an average of 239,000 to 610,000 residents. The low-medium elasticity cities had a net population growth of only 24 percent during the 40 years. After expansion in the early decades, all but Dallas and Columbus are now declining in population as their annexations have slowed or ceased. However, the zero elasticity group has lost population steadily since 1950. As a group, the cities have *lost* 33 percent of their 1950 population. In fact, by 1990, the zero elasticity cities averaged smaller populations (465,000 residents) than either of the other two group cities. Zero elasticity Baltimore City dropped 23 percent from 950,000 residents in 1950 to only 736,000 in 1990.

The explanation for these dramatic differences in different cities' population growth is apparent. In an era of universal, suburban-style growth and smaller household size, cities lost population because

a. they had little or no vacant land on which to develop new, low-density, single-family home subdivisions;

b. they failed to acquire additional vacant land for new subdivision development through annexation or city-county consolidation; and

c. they failed to incorporate newly built suburban communities into their municipality through annexation or consolidation.

TABLE 1.4

Population growth of 22 central cities summarized by
elasticity grouping and compared to Baltimore City
(population in 1,000s)

Classification	City Population, 1950	City Population, 1990	City Population Change	City Population % Growth
Zero elasticity	693	465	−228	−33%
Baltimore City	**950**	**736**	**−214**	**−23%**
Low-medium elasticity	373	462	+89	24%
High-hyper elasticity	239	610	+371	155%

Baltimoreans, so the local tradition holds, are historically slow to embrace change. Examples abound: Large-scale civic projects are introduced, then actively resisted, then, in time, warmly accepted.

The Bay Bridge, the Civic Center, the Jones Falls Expressway, the Beltway, the subway, the many shopping centers, the Orleans Street Viaduct, the National Aquarium, Harborplace itself—all were initially opposed by the electorate. Each was an idea that had to wait until its time had come.

Brief histories of some of Baltimore's high-profile and controversial public-private projects that came into being the hard way are scattered throughout this report. When read together, they make the same point: Despite the popular belief that Baltimore does not take easily to change, Baltimore has changed very much and is continuing to change—and in broad, positive ways.

THE BAY BRIDGE

After Half a Century of Community Resistance, It Finally Got Built in 1952. Some Critics Predicted, "It Would Snap in Two in the Bay's Ice."

For 200 years, as long as there had been an Eastern Shore and a Western Shore, there had been ferries taking people across the water—and talk about a bridge over it.

But it was not until 1907 that Baltimore merchant Peter J. Campbell actually came up with a plan for the bridge. It called for extending Baltimore's streetcar lines beyond their terminal at Bay Shore on the Western Shore over to destinations on the Eastern Shore. Under Campbell's plan, trolley lines would fan out to dozens of towns. But with the growth of the automobile the project died.

In 1916 a group of businessmen got the General Assembly to pass an act authorizing the State Roads Commission to establish a ferry system between Claiborne on the Eastern Shore and Annapolis. In 1919 the ferry "Governor Harrington" began the run, thus inaugurating ferry service across the bay that was to be a way of life for Marylanders for the next 33 years.

In the years from the 1920s to the 1950s there were at least five ways to get across:

- The Love Point Ferry, from Baltimore Harbor to Love Point on the northwestern tip of Kent Island.
- The Claiborne-Annapolis

Continued on page 10

CAPTURE OR CONTRIBUTE?

Table 1.5 compares changes in metro area population with changes in city population to calculate a central city's capture/contribute ratio. The first column calculates the new home population in the metro area from 1950 to 1990. New home population is the sum of the metro area's net population growth plus the loss of population by the central city. (Where the central city has not lost population from 1950 levels, new home population is simply net metro population growth.)

The central city's net population change is then divided by new home population to produce a central city's capture/contribute ratio. In effect, the capture/contribute ratio is a central city's score in the competition for new household formation with its suburbs.

As Table 1.5 demonstrates, zero elasticity cities were net contributors to their suburban growth. They contributed an average of 228,000 residents, or 21 percent, to their suburban population growth. Baltimore contributed 19 percent to its suburban population growth.

Low-medium elasticity cities present a mixed picture, as is fitting for a transitional category. As a group, they captured 10 percent of metro area growth. However, three cities (New Orleans, Louisville, and Richmond) were net contributors. Five cities captured suburban growth—Columbus and Dallas captured a substantial 40 percent and 32 percent, respectively. (By 1994, Norfolk and Atlanta, whose populations have been steadily declining over the last two decades, had slipped into the net contributor category.)

All high-hyper elasticity cities have captured substantial percentages of their metro areas' growth—as a group, a 48 percent share. However, even this impressive performance is understated because of a technicality in the census definition of metro area

TABLE 1.5
City capture/contribute ratios (1950–1990)
(population in 1,000s)

Classification	New Home Population, 1950–1990	City Population Change, 1950–1990	Capture/ Contribute Ratio
Zero elasticity	1,082	−228	−21%
Baltimore City	**1,124**	**−214**	**−19%**
Low-medium elasticity	922	89	10%
High-hyper elasticity	771	371	48%

THE BAY BRIDGE
(continued)

Ferry from 1919 to 1926, which became

- The Annapolis-Matapeake Ferry (later, moved to Sandy Point) from 1926 to the end of ferry service across the bay.
- Baltimore to Tolchester, via the Tolchester boats.
- The "up and around" way—a drive over bad roads via Elkton to Cecil County.

People who rode those ferries recall them now with a certain fondness: they forget the long delays, the heat and the cold, the endless wait in line to board the ferries. Those same persons, sitting in their cars waiting for the ferry, and on board staring out at the distant shore, would curse the system, or the lack of one, and talk about "the bridge." Would it ever be built? And where?

It would be Oct. 1, 1949, before the State Roads Commission would announce that work on the Bay Bridge was at long last beginning. Behind that announcement lay a quarter century's wrangling over location (Sandy Point to Matapeake? Sandy Point to Kent Island? Miller Island to Tolchester?) and the controversy over whether the bridge should be built at all. ("It will turn the Eastern Shore into a Coney Island!" "It will kill marine life?" "It will snap in two in the ice!")

Still on July 30, 1952, Governor Theodore R. McKeldin and former Governor Preston Lane cut the ribbon presenting the bridge formally to Maryland and the world in all its soaring majesty— nothing less than the third longest over-water span in the world. Its traffic capacity on that opening day was said to be 1,500 vehicles an hour in one direction. That "1,500 vehicles an hour" figure is where the trouble began.

In the early 1950s a new phrase had been added to the language in Maryland: "Back-up at the Bay Bridge." By 1963 the bridge was carrying exactly double the number of cars as when it opened, and cries of "Build a second bay bridge!" were heard. Three locations were debated: Miller Island to Tolchester, Calvert County to Dorchester County, and a parallel bridge. Governor Millard Tawes created a commission; it argued for a parallel bridge. But the electorate reacted negatively; it did not want a second bay bridge— anywhere. The matter was petitioned to referendum and the state was set for one of the most

Continued on page 12

boundaries. Greensboro (25 percent) and Raleigh (33 percent) have had seemingly lower capture ratios. However, these cities' scores are affected by the Census Bureau's having combined previously separate metro areas. In fact, Greensboro has captured 60 percent of population growth in Guilford County, and Raleigh has captured 50 percent in Wake County.

Before examining the social and economic consequences of elasticity and inelasticity, a brief discussion of why some cities were elastic and others were inelastic is necessary.

GOOD LAWS, BAD LAWS

Whether or not the cities in this study were able to expand their boundaries during the past four decades depended on three factors:

1. Did state law make annexation easy, difficult, or impossible?
2. Was the city already surrounded by smaller, incorporated municipalities?
3. As an alternative to piecemeal annexation, did state law facilitate city-county consolidation?

State annexation laws vary widely. Since reforming its annexation laws in 1959, North Carolina has had the nation's most liberal annexation statutes. "That which is rural is county, and that which is urban is city" is the North Carolina legislature's policy. North Carolina cities have the power to annex all industrial, commercial, and urbanizing residential property by direct council action regardless of property owners' preferences. In fact, many North Carolina cities exercise extraterritorial zoning powers up to five miles from their city limits and can veto the incorporation of any other municipality within that zone. As a result, Charlotte, Raleigh, and Greensboro have all annexed aggressively and are among the most elastic cities.

By contrast, New Jersey's annexation laws, though on the statute books, are, in practical terms, dead letters. The state's entire territory is divided among 320 incorporated municipalities and 247 incorporated towns. With approval required by all parties affected, boundary changes no longer occur in New Jersey. New Jersey's political geography is fixed and immutable (as, in effect, are those of New York, Pennsylvania, and all of New England). In fact, requiring either other jurisdictions or local property owners to approve an annexation is typically a death knell for a city's annexation hopes.

Within the same state, history can deal different cities a different hand. As older, mature cities, by 1950, Cleveland and Cincin-

THE BAY BRIDGE
(continued)

interesting legislative performances in the history of Maryland politics.

1967: Governor Spiro T. Agnew revived the parallel span issue; authorization was approved as an emergency measure, coupled with future northern and southern crossings and a second Baltimore Harbor Tunnel. The State Roads commission was to decide which project would go first. To the surprise of few, it selected the parallel bridge.

1973: Governor Marvin Mandel and Mrs. William Preston Lane cut the ribbon at the toll plaza on the western end of the parallel bridge. Mandel paid the $1 toll to Maryland Transportation Secretary Harry R. Hughes.

It has been over 40 years since the first bridge opened, almost 25 since the second opened—and almost 90 years since Peter J. Campbell advanced his quaint theory that by extending Baltimore's streetcar line across the bay, "Baltimore," as he put it then, "would be opening its rich marketplace to all of the people on the Eastern Shore."

For all his vision, he never dreamed that in terms of opening a "rich marketplace" the bridge would work both ways.

---

nati were already completely surrounded by other, incorporated suburban communities. They could not expand their boundaries. By contrast, Columbus was a younger community that was not yet hemmed in by smaller municipalities. Columbus launched a policy of aggressive annexation. City leaders were motivated by two goals: First, never allow Columbus to be completely surrounded by incorporated suburbs. Second, through annexation, become Ohio's most populous city (which Columbus did, surpassing Cincinnati by the mid-1960s and Cleveland by the mid-1980s).

Finally, Nashville, Jacksonville, and Indianapolis all became highly elastic by consolidating with their surrounding counties (as will be discussed).

Baltimore City's inelasticity became, in essence, absolute in 1948. By a 57 percent to 43 percent statewide margin, suburban foes of Baltimore City's renewed expansion passed a constitutional amendment, preventing Baltimore City from annexing any part of its surrounding counties without the approval of affected citizens. Baltimore City's long-term fate was sealed by that action, since it is unlikely that the affected citizens would today approve any annexation.

There were many motivations for suburban resistance to central city annexation. Most Americans believe in local home rule: The more local (and smaller) the government, the better. Beyond the pull of better suburban housing values, better suburban schools, and safer suburban neighborhoods, many ex-city dwellers were fleeing higher city taxes and city politics.

In many metro areas, including Baltimore, racially motivated "white flight" was undeniably a major factor. In the 1950s and 1960s, "good" neighborhoods with "good" schools often were seen as neighborhoods and schools without any blacks. After the civil rights revolution, neighborhoods and schools without *poor* blacks met the "good" test. Economic segregation—with heavy racial and ethnic overtones—has increased in urban America.

Racial prejudice played a significant role in the evolution of overwhelmingly white suburbs surrounding increasingly black cities. How strong a role can be debated, but the demographic, social, and economic consequences of central city inelasticity have become clear over the past 40 years.

URBAN APARTHEID

Table 1.6 relates urban elasticity to racial distribution by residence. Each of the three groups of metro areas has about the same average black population metro-wide (20 percent, 21 percent, and 19 percent, respectively). Zero-elastic cities, however, have much higher black populations (51 percent) than low-medium elastic cities (42 percent) or high-hyper elastic cities (27 percent). This phenomenon is not just the mathematical result of enlarging the denominator (i.e., the central city's share of areawide population). On a neighborhood-by-neighborhood basis, more elastic areas are less racially segregated than inelastic areas.

TABLE 1.6
Racial composition and racial segregation in 22 metro areas in 1990

Classification	Metro % Black Population, 1990	City % Black Population, 1990	Neighborhood Segregation Index	Public School Segregation Index
Zero elasticity	20%	51%	75	74
Baltimore Metro	**26%**	**59%**	71	67
Low-medium elasticity	21%	42%	65	59
High-hyper elasticity	19%	27%	60	46

The third column in Table 1.6 summarizes the results of Census Bureau calculations of residential racial segregation. The measure used is the "Taueber index" or "dissimilarity index" that is commonly used by demographers. It is a measure of the relative evenness or unevenness of the distribution of the black population across all census tracts in a metropolitan area. On this scale, 0 would be a completely even distribution (i.e., complete integration), and 100 would be a completely uneven distribution (i.e., complete segregation). What this statistic means, for example, is that in the Baltimore region, 71 percent of all blacks would have to move into other neighborhoods (in the mathematically correct proportions) to have an even distribution of blacks (26 percent) in all neighborhoods.

Thus, for zero elasticity metro areas, the black residential segregation index is 75; for low-medium elasticity metro areas, 65; and for high-hyper elasticity metro areas, 60.

School segregation follows a similar pattern. The fourth column summarizes the evenness of distribution of black high school students throughout all public school systems in each metro area. For zero elasticity metro areas, the black school segregation index is 74 (for metro Baltimore, 67); for low-medium elasticity metro areas, 59; and for high-hyper elasticity metro areas, 46. School segregation scores are better (that is, lower) for two reasons. First, high school attendance zones are typically larger than census tracts; analyzing school enrollment patterns by elementary schools would bring measures of residential segregation and measures of school segregation closer together. More important, many of the more elastic metro areas are southern and border state communities whose large, sometimes countywide school systems are under federal desegregation plans. Southern classrooms are more integrated than southern neighborhoods.

Economic segregation follows patterns similar to those of racial segregation. Table 1.7 measures economic disparities on a jurisdictional level—the (nominal) per capita income by central city and suburban area. In 1989, zero elasticity areas have the highest metro-wide incomes ($17,340)[4] and the highest suburban incomes ($18,785) but the lowest city incomes ($12,511, or $11,449 without Washington, D.C.). For zero elasticity cities, average city incomes are only 67 percent of average suburban incomes.

---

[4]The zero elasticity metro area's higher income levels are an illusion, because census data is not adjusted for area-by-area differences in cost of living. See the discussion beginning on page 36.

TABLE 1.7
Nominal per capita income disparity between city and suburbs
(nominal per capita income)

Classification	Metro per capita Income, 1989	City per capita Income, 1989	Suburban per capita Income, 1989	City Suburban Income Ratio
Zero elasticity	$17,340	$12,511	$18,795	67%
Baltimore Metro	**$16,596**	**$11,994**	**$18,660**	**64%**
Low-medium elasticity	$14,748	$13,384	$15,658	85%
High-hyper elasticity	$14,904	$15,175	$15,211	100%

At the other end of the scale, the high-hyper elasticity areas have the second highest metro incomes ($14,904), the highest city incomes ($15,175), and the lowest suburban incomes ($15,211). Their average city incomes are equal to average suburban incomes (100 percent).[5]

The economic gap is further emphasized in Table 1.8, which depicts the distribution of poor people. As metro areas, all groups have about the same proportion (nominally) of poor people—10 percent, 12 percent, and 11 percent, respectively. However, 23 percent and 22 percent of the residents of the more inelastic cities are poor, contrasted with only 13 percent of the high-hyper elasticity cities.

While this is a measure that is affected by change in the mathematical denominator, the significance for city hall is best measured by a city's fair share poverty index. This is a measure of a city's share of the metro area's poor compared with its share of all residents of the metro area. An index of 100 means that a city's share of the poor population is neither more nor less than the proportion of poor people within the whole metro community.

By this measure, zero elasticity cities have more than twice their fair share of their metro areas' poor (238 percent). Baltimore City is just under the group average at 217 percent. By contrast, low-medium elasticity cities have less than twice their fair share (180 percent), while high-hyper elasticity cities have close to their fair share (120 percent).

Table 1.8 explains, in briefest terms, the basic reason why inelastic central cities are failing: They have too many poor residents

---

[5]In many metro areas, there are secondary central cities whose incomes have been excluded from calculations of suburban incomes. This explains, for example, why metro-wide average income does not always fall within the bounds of the central city and suburban average incomes.

TABLE 1.8
Distribution of poor residents between city and suburbs

Classification	Metro % Poverty, 1990	City % Poverty, 1990	City Fair Share Poverty
Zero elasticity	10%	23%	238%
Baltimore City	**10%**	**22%**	**217%**
Low-medium elasticity	12%	22%	180%
High-hyper elasticity	11%	13%	120%

to succeed. Such communities face spiraling costs to serve the poor. Yet because such a high poverty rate reflects the abandonment of the city by middle class residents, the city tax base is shrinking relative to needs.

BLUE COLLAR, WHITE COLLAR

Compounding the impact of these population trends are vast transformations that are underway in the American economy. The "deindustrialization" of the American economy has been studied by many. Table 1.9 measures changes in manufacturing employment between 1973 and 1988. During this 15-year period, the share of national earnings generated by manufacturing dropped from 25 percent to 20 percent; in net employment, manufacturing dropped almost 500,000 jobs—a 2.3 percent total decline. Over this period, the Baltimore metro area lost 45,800 factory jobs, or 25 percent of its total manufacturing employment.

TABLE 1.9
Changes in manufacturing employment between 1973 and 1988
(jobs in 1,000s)

Classification	Metro Manufacturing Jobs, 1973	Metro Manufacturing Jobs, 1988	Metro Manufacturing Jobs Change
Zero elasticity	24%	15%	−16%
Baltimore	**18%**	**10%**	**−25%**
Low-medium elasticity	18%	12%	−1%
High-hyper elasticity	22%	16%	12%

The impact of deindustrialization has varied among different types of metropolitan areas (and in different regions of the country). In 1973, all three elasticity groups had roughly the same manufacturing base (between 19 percent and 24 percent of all jobs). Over the next 15 years, zero elasticity areas lost 15 percent of their manufacturing jobs, while (despite mixed experience) low-medium elasticity areas almost broke even. With only Indianapolis recording manufacturing losses, high-hyper elasticity areas gained 12 percent in manufacturing employment.

By the early 1970s, factory employment had been shifting gradually from the industrial Northeast and Middle West to Southern and Western states. Since most zero elasticity communities are located in Frostbelt regions and most high-hyper elastic communities are located in the Sunbelt, this regional shift in manufacturing employment was being reflected in the economic mix of each group well before the 1970s. In all communities, however, the manufacturing sector's importance had declined by 1988.

Deindustrialization of the overall U.S. economy did not begin until the 1970s when the American market opened increasingly to imports of goods from resurgent Japan and Western Europe. In the 1950s and 1960s, manufacturing did decline steadily *in relative importance*. In 1950, manufacturing accounted for 31 percent of all employment; factory jobs had declined to 25 percent by 1973. However, during those two decades, almost all metro areas experienced *absolute increases* in manufacturing employment, including all our sample communities, as summarized in the first column of Table 1.10. From 1950 to 1973, factory jobs *increased* by 14 percent in zero elasticity metro areas and by over 80 per-

TABLE 1.10
Manufacturing employment, population change, and city-to-suburb income ratio between 1950 and 1990

Classification	Metro Factory Jobs, 1950–1973	Metro Factory Jobs, 1973–1988	City Population Change, 1950–1970	City/ Metro Income Ratio, 1950	City/ Metro Income Ratio, 1990
Zero elasticity	14%	−16%	−12%	93%	70%
Baltimore City	**9%**	**−25%**	**−5%**	**98%**	**73%**
Low-medium elasticity	83%	−1%	30%	99%	76%
High-hyper elasticity	82%	12%	108%	102%	95%

HARBORPLACE ALMOST *DIDN'T* GET BUILT!

It Was Saved by Only 16,317 Votes! Many Predicted the Worst if It Got Built: "Hordes Will Descend on This Place and Destroy It!"

It is the conventional wisdom in Baltimore that Harborplace marked the beginning of an era; a door slammed shut on the old Baltimore and opened on the new—not only on a physical landscape of tall buildings and lovely waterside plazas, but onto vistas of unlimited growth and unrestrained optimism.

You would think that so large and meaningful a public project ($16 million worth of it) and all calculated to rejuvenate the sixth largest city in America would be, in the record of history, a citizenry's well-ordered march to glory. But the coming about of Harborplace was no such thing. It almost didn't happen.

The whole undertaking—all the glitter and the glass and the tourism and the hotels and the conventions—all of it turned on the mood and the mind and the vote of only 16,317 people.

And we don't even know who they were. When, in November of 1978, the question of whether Harborplace was to be built, 59,045 voted for Harborplace, but 42,728 voted against it. Those scant 16,317 voters who made the difference are the unsung heroes of Baltimore. Their choice, in retrospect, may have seemed to be an easy one to make, but it wasn't. In 1978 the notions of developing the Inner Harbor in general and of building Harborplace in particular were cast in the fiery furnace of controversy.

"We don't want any Harborplace!," a coalition of community improvement associations screamed. "Hordes will descend upon this place of incomparable beauty and destroy it!"

"Utterly ridiculous!" was the loud and forceful response from the Citizens For Harborplace: "It'll be like having a City Fair every day of the year!"

Tempers flared at the public hearing where the plans were presented. Both sides had lined up authoritative endorsements for their respective points of view. But in the end, the anti's had succeeded in getting the 12,000 signatures required to bring the question to the voters. And from that day until election day the papers were full of partisan letters-to-editor, and the radio talk shows heard these same points of view non-stop.

But the clock was running, and on election day 99,703 Baltimoreans on both sides of the issue and from all 503 precincts went into the voting booths for a

Continued on page 20

cent within the more elastic communities. During this same period of modest overall industrial growth, zero elasticity cities were already losing population to their new suburbs (–12 percent), and the income gap was widening. Median family income of inelastic city residents dropped from 93 percent to 70 percent of the metropolitan average.

In short, the catastrophic loss of factory jobs in the last two decades hit hardest at older, industrial communities. It closed off many traditional paths of economic and social mobility for millions of unskilled and semiskilled workers—many of whom were minorities in inner-city neighborhoods. It undoubtedly magnified the economic disparities between older cities and newer suburbs. However, deindustrialization intensified *but did not create* the severe racial and economic isolation that today characterizes inelastic cities and their surrounding areas.

While blue collar occupations declined in importance, information-based white collar occupations flourished. Table 1.11 shows that employment in finance, insurance, and real estate (the so-called "FIRE" occupational category) expanded rapidly in all metro areas—65 percent, 70 percent, and 81 percent among the three elasticity groupings. Nationally, employment in FIRE occupations increased 74 percent during this period, while earnings in FIRE went up even more rapidly (81 percent).

The services occupations have been the leading growth sector of the postindustrial era. The services sector's share of the national economy increased from 16 percent in 1973 to over 24 percent in 1988 as the result of overall growth rate of 109 percent in earn-

TABLE 1.11
Change in employment for manufacturing, service, and FIRE (finance, insurance, and real estate) for 22 metro areas between 1973 and 1988 summarized by elasticity grouping and compared to Baltimore (population in 1,000s)

Classification	Metro Manufacturing Jobs Change, 1973–1988	Metro FIRE Jobs Change, 1973–1988	Metro Service Jobs, 1973–1988	Metro All Jobs Change, 1973–1988
Zero elasticity	–16%	65%	83%	33%
Baltimore Metro	**–25%**	**77%**	**92%**	**33%**
Low-medium elasticity	–1%	70%	93%	46%
High-hyper elasticity	12%	81%	109%	55%

HARBORPLACE ALMOST *DIDN'T* GET BUILT!
(continued)

rendezvous with history. When they emerged, they had made some.

Harborplace is now enjoyed by so many that it is written up and spoken of all over the world. The glamorous complex is held up as one of the great urban success stories in the country. It has made Baltimore more attractive to industry, to tourists, and to Baltimoreans themselves. It has spurred a stunning boom in real estate.

Against the odds.

---

ings.[6] National employment in services occupations grew 85 percent, increasing their share of the national work force from under 20 percent to 26 percent.

Among the three elasticity categories, the services sector increased vigorously. Led by the Washington metro area's spectacular 124 percent growth rate, services jobs increased 83 percent for the zero elasticity group. (Metro Baltimore's growth rate in services occupations was 92 percent.) Paced by Atlanta (129 percent) and Dallas (130 percent), the low-medium elasticity group increased services employment by 95 percent. All high-hyper elasticity metro areas experienced high growth rates in services, averaging 109 percent.

The net effect of all these trends is summarized in the last column of Table 1.11. While national employment grew 37 percent over the 15 years, the zero elasticity metro areas (including Baltimore) fell short of the national average (33 percent). Again paced by spectacular expansion in metro Atlanta and metro Dallas, the job supply in the low-medium elasticity group expanded 46 percent. With Raleigh-Durham as the flagship economy (81 percent), overall job growth in the high-hyper elasticity group averaged 55 percent.

This shift in employment patterns has worked against many inner-city residents. New job creation in downtown business districts has emphasized professional and other high-skill office occupations that are beyond the education and skill levels of many inner-city residents. Lower-wage, lower-skill retail and service jobs have expanded primarily in the suburbs, where the bulk of con-

---

[6]Included in the services sector, for example, are all private health occupations.

sumers are located. Many inner-city residents have limited access to suburban-based jobs they can perform, lacking both affordable transportation and personal networks to link them to suburban employment opportunities.

Thus, most of the better jobs being created within central cities are held by suburban commuters, while many of the jobs generated by the suburbs are beyond the reach of inner-city residents. Income gaps between city residents and suburban residents continue to grow.

THE POINT OF NO RETURN

In my research, I have identified a critical "point of no return" past which central cities continue inexorably to slide downward economically, socially, and fiscally. That point of no return is defined by three threshold indicators for central cities:

    a. population loss, typically 20 percent or more from peak levels;

    b. a *disproportionate* minority population, typically a 30 percent or more black and Hispanic population that is at least twice (i.e., 2.0) the metropolitan percentage of minorities;

    c. most critically, a city/suburban per capita income ratio of 70 percent or less.

Table 1.12 lists all central cities that have passed the point of no return. The principal central city of a metro area is listed in capital letters (for example, NEWARK, NJ). A secondary central city in a metro area is listed in lowercase letters (e.g., East St. Louis, IL).

First, the table reveals that almost all cities have lost substantial populations. Those that have slowed their population slide or have recently regained population slightly (e.g., Bridgeport, Paterson, Hartford) have done so through substantial Hispanic immigration, which has added, if anything, to the cities, substantial social welfare burdens. Second, all cities have continued to increase their percentage of minority residents.

But most significantly, all cities have continued to decline in income relative to their suburbs. Over the last decade, the widening of the income gap has ranged from a low of –4 percent (in Baltimore, for example) to –18 percent (Petersburg, Va.). However, for all cities past the point of no return, growing economic disparities have been universal. *No city that has passed the point of no return has ever closed the economic gap on its suburbs by as much as one percentage point!*

TABLE 1.12
34 central cities have passed the point of no return by exceeding
threshold indicators in at least two of three categories

	Population Loss by 1990 (greater than 20%)	Disproportionate Minority Population in 1990 (greater than 30%)	City/Metro Minority Ratio	City-to-Suburb Income Ratio (less than 70%)
Holyoke, MA	−26%	35%	2.4	69%
BIRMINGHAM, AL	−22%	64%	2.3	69%
FLINT, MI	−29%	52%	2.3	69%
BUFFALO, NY	−43%	37%	2.6	69%
ST. LOUIS, MO	−54%	50%	2.6	67%
CHICAGO, IL	−23%	60%	1.7	66%
SAGINAW, MI	−29%	50%	3.6	66%
BALTIMORE, MD	**−23%**	**60%**	**2.2**	**64%**
DAYTON, OH	−31%	36%	2.9	64%
PHILADELPHIA, PA	−23%	45%	2.0	64%
YOUNGSTOWN, OH	−44%	35%	3.3	64%
Kansas City, KS	−11%	38%	2.4	63%
Petersburg, VA	−7%	74%	2.5	63%
NEW HAVEN, CT	−21%	47%	2.9	62%
MILWAUKEE, WI*	−15%	39%	2.1	62%
ATLANTIC CITY, NJ	−43%	69%	3.3	61%
East Chicago, IN	−41%	81%	3.0	60%
GARY, IN	−25%	85%	3.1	59%
Bessemer, AL	−11%	59%	2.1	58%
Chicago Heights, IL*	−19%	50%	1.5	57%
Pontiac, MI*	−17%	52%	2.2	55%
Elizabeth, NJ*	−4%	60%	1.8	54%
CLEVELAND, OH	−45%	50%	2.4	54%
Perth Amboy, NJ*	−4%	60%	4.7	53%
HARTFORD, CT	−21%	66%	4.4	53%
DETROIT, MI	−44%	77%	3.3	53%
TRENTON, NJ	−31%	59%	2.5	50%
PATERSON, NJ*	−3%	72%	3.7	47%
BENTON HARBOR, MI	−33%	93%	5.4	43%
NEWARK, NJ	−38%	82%	2.4	42%
BRIDGEPORT, CT*	−11%	50%	2.8	41%
North Chicago, IL	−26%	47%	3.3	39%
Camden, NJ	−30%	86%	3.8	39%
East St. Louis, IL	−50%	98%	5.3	39%

*Loss of population has been slowed by heavy Hispanic immigration in Milwaukee, Chicago Heights, Pontiac, Bridgeport, Elizabeth, Perth Amboy, and Paterson.

WHY SHOULD SUBURBS CARE?

Why should suburbs care if central cities are failing? Aren't suburbs doing just fine? Isn't this a new type of evolving urban form, where suburbanites can be independent of and sealed off from the problems of their core cities?

The answer is "no." In many ways, suburbs pay for the cost of dying cities:

- Suburbs pay through higher state and federal taxes to support increased social services and urban aid. These costs impose a heavy burden on a region's competitive position.
- Suburbs pay for costly duplication of major regional facilities when suburbanites no longer feel comfortable and secure in using city-based facilities. What other society in the world regularly abandons a previous generation's investment to build anew?
- Suburbanites pay in sacrificing their enjoyment of a region's history and tradition. What is distinctive about a region are the neighborhoods and civic facilities that are most often found in its cities, not in its suburbs. Everybody's suburban shopping mall looks like everybody else's. (At least they all have the same stores.)

Many suburbanites may be willing to pay the costs to maintain the illusion of their isolation from inner-city problems. But they pay another price as well—reduced prosperity for themselves today and for their children tomorrow.

The strongest regions economically generally have strong central cities at their core. The healthiest suburbs typically exist around healthy central cities.

Table 1.13 shows the growth in real family income over the past four decades. The growth of nominal median family income from 1949 to 1989 has been calculated, and two adjustments have been made for changes in the cost of living. First, the growth rate was adjusted to reflect changes in the national Consumer Price Index. Second, a further adjustment was made to reflect changes in the

TABLE 1.13
Adjusted growth in real family income, 1949–1989

Classification	Growth in Metro Real Income, 1949–1989	Growth in City Real Income, 1949–1989
Zero elasticity	129%	56%
Baltimore	**145%**	**68%**
Low-medium elasticity	134%	72%
High-hyper elasticity	149%	119%

FIGURE 1.1
Growth in real median family income for 277 metro areas and
central cities from 1949–1989

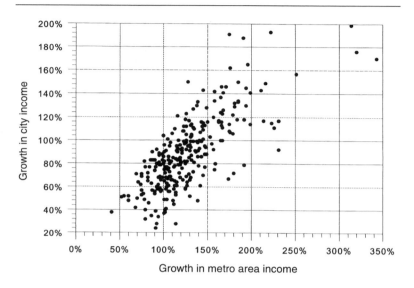

relative cost of living for each metro area for 1950 and 1990, compared to the national metro average.

Metro Baltimore has had a strong economic performance over
the past 40 years. Its growth rate in real family income has been 145
percent; the real standard of living for the typical Baltimore area
family more than doubled. For the 22 metro areas, that growth in
real income is equaled or exceeded only by Charlotte, Greensboro,
Jacksonville, Richmond, Washington, D.C., Nashville, Atlanta, and
Raleigh. All these metro areas, however, have had more vigorous
rates of income growth in their central cities. Among the 22 cities
themselves, Baltimore City's growth rate (68 percent) ranks 15th.

To place the relationship between city economic growth in an
even broader context, Figure 1.1 relates the growth in real median
family income for all central cities in 277 metro areas.[7] The growth
in central city real median family income is charted on the vertical
axis; the growth of metro-wide real median family income is
charted on the horizontal axis.

---

[7]The author's study covers 522 central cities, 254 Metropolitan Statistical Areas (MSAs), and
17 Consolidated Metropolitan Areas (NECMAs). Eight areas are omitted from the scattergram because of data gaps or because they are, in effect, "Mexican border towns" whose dynamics are profoundly different from those of the rest of the country.

TABLE 1.14
Adjusted growth in real per capita income

Classification	Growth in Metro Real Income, 1969–1989	Growth in City Real Income, 1969–1989	Growth in Suburban Real Income, 1969–1989
Zero elasticity	41%	19%	47%
Baltimore	**49%**	**23%**	**61%**
Low-medium elasticity	38%	28%	43%
High-hyper elasticity	45%	40%	49%

For 504 central cities, the average rate of growth in family income is 89 percent. For their 277 metro areas, the average rate of growth is 128 percent. The scattergram shows a solid, positive relationship between city income growth and metro income growth.[8]

Table 1.14 takes a look at a closer period of time (1969–1989). It summarizes the 20-year growth of real *per capita* income rather than real median family income as analyzed in Table 1.13 and Figure 1.1. (Per capita income gives more weight to wealthy individuals than does median family income.) Furthermore, the income growth rates in Table 1.14 have been adjusted only for changes in the national Consumer Price Index for this 20-year period, since I have not calculated metro area costs of living for 1970.

As metro areas, the zero-elastic group performed well; regional real incomes per capita increased 41 percent over the 20 years. The sample group does split into two sections. Postindustrial, service-based economies—Washington (50 percent), Newark (in Manhattan's shadow—49 percent), Baltimore (49 percent), and Oakland (50 percent)—did well. Metro areas still grappling with loss of industrial jobs—Cleveland (23 percent), St. Louis (35 percent), and Cincinnati (35 percent)—did less well.

The low-medium elasticity group (a 37 percent increase) showed somewhat the same dichotomy (e.g., more industrial Louisville 30 percent versus postindustrial Atlanta 49 percent). Among the high-hyper elasticity group (a 45 percent increase overall), more industrial Indianapolis (32 percent) lagged while research triangle Raleigh-Durham (62 percent) led the pack.

---

[8]The coefficient of correlation, or statistical "fit," between city income growth (the "independent" variable) and metro income growth (the dependent variable) is 0.56. City income growth, of course, is not truely independent of metro income growth.

However, as further shown by Table 1.14, the distribution of growth in real income varied greatly between city residents and suburban residents in the different elasticity categories. While in zero-elastic metro areas suburbanites' real incomes grew by 47 percent, the real incomes of city residents grew by only 19 percent. Indeed, at 23 percent "real" growth in per capita income, Baltimore City ranked second only to Washington, D.C. (45 percent) among the seven zero elastic cities.

By contrast, low-medium elastic cities had growth rates in real income that were 50 percent greater (i.e., 28 percent to 19 percent) than those of the zero elastic cities. And high-hyper elastic cities had twice the rate of growth in real incomes (40 percent) of zero-elastic cities, and high-hyper elastic metro areas had the highest growth rates of any metro areas (45 percent).

THE *REAL* STANDARD OF LIVING

There is another important question that must be answered by using cost-of-living indicators—what are the *real* standards-of-living in metro Baltimore and Baltimore City today?

The introduction noted that the 1990 census ranked the Baltimore area 20th in the nation in per capita income (and metro Washington ranked first!). However, the census reports local income as if a dollar has the same buying power throughout the country. That simply is not true. The San Francisco, California area is much more expensive (cost-of-living index: 183) than Pine Bluff, Arkansas (cost-of-living index: 75). How does metro Baltimore compare with other metro areas?

The cost-of-living index (1989) is measurably higher in the zero-elastic metro areas (120 percent) than in the low-medium elastic areas (98 percent) or high-hyper elastic areas (97 percent). (For metro Baltimore, the index is 110 percent—that is, the Baltimore area's cost of living was 10 percent above the national metro average in 1989.) Using these indices to adjust the 1989 per capita income figures presented in Table 1.7 produces some revealing adjustments (Table 1.15).

From having the highest *nominal* per capita income for metro areas ($17,340), the zero elasticity group drops to the lowest *real* per capita income ($14,741) while the high-hyper elasticity metro areas (nominal income: $14,904) edge upward into the lead (real income: $15,443).

More significant is the impact of these adjustments on central city per capita incomes (*if* the metro-wide cost-of-living indices are

TABLE 1.15
Per capita income disparity between metro area and city,
adjusted for cost of living, in 22 metro areas, summarized by
elasticity grouping and compared to metro Baltimore

Classification	Metro COLA Adjust, 1989	Metro Nominal Income, 1989	Metro Adjusted Income, 1989	City Nominal Income, 1989	City Adjusted Income, 1989
Zero elasticity	120%	$17,340	$14,741	$12,511	$10,671
Baltimore	**110%**	**$16,596**	**$15,087**	**$11,994**	**$10,904**
Low-medium elasticity	98%	$14,748	$15,129	$13,384	$13,713
High-hyper elasticity	97%	$14,904	$15,443	$15,175	$15,730

equally applicable to central city living). Thus adjusted, real per capita income levels in zero elasticity cities fall to $10,671, farther behind low-medium elasticity cities ($13,713) and high-hyper elasticity cities ($15,730). In summary, the real standard of living of residents of zero elasticity cities is 22 percent and 32 percent below the real standard of living of residents of low-medium and high-hyper elasticity cities, respectively.

For the Baltimore area, these adjustments drop metro-wide per capital income from a glittering if nominal $16,596 (fifth highest) to a more modest but real $15,087 (16th highest). Baltimore City income drops from a nominal $11,994 (16th) to a real $10,904 (18th out of 21 adjusted).

These are just comparisons of real per capita income among the 22 metro areas paired with metro Baltimore. If we apply the same adjustment for cost of living to rankings by median family income for all 320 metro areas, metro Baltimore falls from 16th place to 76th.[9] Baltimore City falls from 185th place to 257th. Even Baltimore suburbs drop from 11th place to 34th in the rankings.

In short, in real-life terms, metro Baltimore isn't doing as well economically as the census report would imply because the census assumes that the dollar has the same buying power all around the country. Adjusted for cost of living, there are approximately 75 metro areas that have a higher standard of living

[9]Metro Baltimore's cost of living index is 110. The cost-of-living index for metro Washington is 137. Applying cost-of-living adjustments to the Washington area's census-reported median family income drops metro Washington from first place to 48th. As a central city, the District of Columbia falls from an impressive 31st place to 244th, while Washington's suburbs (minus Arlington County and Frederick, Maryland) fall from first place to 69th!

than metro Baltimore. There are over 30 other suburban areas with higher standards of living than suburban Baltimore. And with its ranking of 257th out of 315 principal central cities (as measured, at least, by real median family income), practically anywhere has a higher real median family income than Baltimore City—except for other "inelastic" cities that are farther down the path of decline.[10]

REGIONAL ECONOMIC GROWTH—
THE CITY'S SALVATION?

Nevertheless, Baltimore City residents did experience real growth in income levels both during the last 20 years (23 percent) and over the past four decades (68 percent). Does this suggest that the argument that Baltimore City is programmed to decline steadily can be dismissed? Can Baltimore City—and its suburbs—look to a continuation of strong economic growth to turn Baltimore City around in the long run?

No, for several reasons. *First,* real economic growth is America's economic norm. Real income levels in all central cities have grown over the last four decades.[11] In some objective sense, America's poorest households are incomparably better off materially than the great majority of residents of many Third World nations and "better off" than their counterparts in past generations.[12] What is relevant for American society is the perception—and the reality—of great disparities of wealth and opportunity within American communities. Such slow, long-term growth in real income as has occurred in Baltimore City is measured only by the economist—not in the eye of the black youth who lives in

---

[10]Some such similar adjustment would also realign slightly the poverty levels reported in Table 1.8. In zero elasticity areas, poverty levels would rise to 11 percent (metro) and 26 percent (city) while remaining at the same levels in the low-medium elasticity areas (12 percent metro, 22 percent city) and high-hyper elasticity areas (11 percent metro, 13 percent city). Metro Baltimore's poverty level would move to 11 percent, and Baltimore City's poverty level would increase to 25 percent.

[11]The lone exception is Benton Harbor, Michigan, where median family incomes in real terms dropped 35 percent between 1950 and 1990. A poor (58 percent), black (92 percent) enclave in the middle of Berrien County, Michigan, Benton Harbor is still world headquarters of the Whirlpool Corporation. Real median family incomes even increased in East St. Louis (6 percent) and Detroit (12 percent). Median family income in Benton Harbor is only two-thirds that of East St. Louis!

[12]As former Atlanta mayor Maynard Jackson has said, "The level of poverty throughout the world is so high that Atlanta's "fair share of poverty index [273]" wasn't even an issue with the International Olympic Committee in awarding the 1996 Olympics to Atlanta!" (from a speech to the Council on Foundation, May 2, 1994, in New York City.)

TABLE 1.16
Place of employment for residents of Howard and Anne Arundel
Counties in 1979 and 1989

County	Work in Own County, 1979	Work in Metro Baltimore, 1979	Work in Metro Washington, 1979	Work in Own County, 1989	Work in Metro Baltimore, 1989	Work in Metro Washington, 1989
Anne Arundel	57%	24%	19%	61%	18%	20%
Howard	34%	33%	31%	36%	31%	32%

the Lafayette Terrace public housing project. Metro Baltimore must address the issue of disparities.

Second, the Baltimore region (as well as metro Washington) was a primary beneficiary of the most powerful regional economic development tool of the 1980s: the federal deficit. I hope that, for the good of the nation, the federal deficit is being brought under control. However, cutting the federal deficit will reduce that source of economic stimulus for the Baltimore economy.

The economic growth of the Baltimore area is not being driven primarily by Baltimore City–based businesses. Suburban Anne Arundel and Howard Counties are leading the surge, and their economic growth is increasingly powered by employment growth generated from within the Washington metro (Table 1.16).

The economic interdependence between metro Baltimore and metro Washington was officially recognized in December 1992 when the federal Office of Management and Budget combined both metro areas into the Washington-Baltimore Consolidated Metropolitan Statistical area (CMSA). With 6.5 million people, the new Washington-Baltimore CMSA is the nation's fourth most populous market area. But make no mistake. It is the Washington segment that is the primary driving force and senior partner. Baltimore City could become more and more an economic backwater within the region.

Third, even within Baltimore City, improvement in incomes is not evenly shared; overall, city incomes went up because higher-income households did very well while the poor got poorer.

Fourth, the number of poverty neighborhoods continues to grow. The growth of slums partially offsets the benefit of new investment downtown in terms of Baltimore City's tax base (see Chapter Three for discussion of these points).

Finally, no other city in Baltimore City's circumstances—past the point of no return—has turned its situation around. What would make Baltimore different?

CHAPTER TWO

THE ALTERNATIVES

This chapter will examine successful strategies in other metropolitan areas for maintaining central cities' elasticity and diminishing racial and economic isolation. (In the next chapter, these different strategies will be evaluated for Baltimore, and a specific course of action for the Baltimore metro area will be recommended.) These strategies can be grouped into three general approaches.

The first approach is to expand the jurisdiction of the central city in response to actual or potential peripheral growth. The most common technique is for the central city to annex additional areas before or in the early stages of development. Much less common is expansion of the city through formal consolidation with another government—typically with its surrounding county government.

The second approach is to create a second tier of government that functions above the network of local governments (municipalities, townships, and counties) but below the level of state government. This second-tier government can then assume powers over the lower-level governments to promote greater social and economic equity.

The third approach forgoes formal reorganization of local government. Instead, it emphasizes creating policies and programs that require existing local governments to act as if they were a unified metropolitan government with a metropolitan-wide constituency. Most important of these are policies and programs that bring about a more even distribution of low-income residents (particularly poor minorities) throughout the metropolitan area. Of secondary importance are policies that share governmental revenues across jurisdictional lines.

STRATEGIES FOR EXPANDING
CENTRAL CITY JURISDICTIONS

1. Annexation

Annexation is the most common method by which central cities have expanded their municipal territory. Table 2.1 summarizes the level of annexation activity in all metro areas decade by decade

TABLE 2.1
Territorial growth of central cities (1950–1990)

	Cities with Annexations	Area Annexed (sq. mi.)	City Area % Growth by Annexing
Total 1950 area—522 cities		10,498	
1950–1960	260	3,299	31%
1960–1970	366	3,893	28%
1970–1980	306	2,726	14%
1980–1990	398	2,625	11%
Total added by annexation		**12,543**	
Total added by mergers		**4,662**	
Percent added by annexation			73%
Percent added by mergers			27%
Total 1990 area—522 cities		**27,703**	
Percent growth in city area—			
1950–1990			164%

since 1950. Over the 40 years, the territory of 522 central cities grew from 10,498 square miles to 27,703 square miles. About 73 percent of this growth (12,543 square miles) came by annexation. In proportional terms, the greatest level of annexation activity occurred during the 1950s and 1960s, when central cities added 31 percent and 28 percent, respectively, to their municipal areas through annexation. Growth by annexation fell proportionally to 14 percent and 11 percent, respectively, in the 1970s and 1980s. (Adding always to a larger base, it is almost inescapable that over time, annexations would add proportionally less.) However, the level of annexation activity remained significant even in these later decades. During the 1980s, 398 central cities (about three-fourths of all central cities) added a total of 2,625 square miles through annexation.

However, during these 40 years, there have been sharp differences region by region in the use of annexation. Table 2.2 shows that the greatest amount of land annexed by central cities has occurred in the 16 Southern states (7,463 square miles, or 57 percent of the total). Second in activity are the 13 Western states (3,240 square miles, or 24.7 percent). Some 2,323 square miles (17.7 percent) have been annexed in the 12 Midwestern states, while annexation activity has been virtually nonexistent in the nine

TABLE 2.2
Annexation by region (1950–1990)

	Area Annexed 1950–1990 (sq. mi.)	% of Total National Annexations
Northeast	72	0.5%
Midwest	2,323	17.7%
West	3,240	24.7%
Arizona	856	6.5%
California	1,284	9.8%
South	7,463	57.0%
Alabama	560	4.3%
Florida	649	5.0%
North Carolina	549	4.2%
Oklahoma	1,201	9.2%
Texas	2,659	20.3%

Northeastern states. (Most variations in the size of Northeastern central cities probably reflect more accurate surveying. The expansion of Danbury, Connecticut, accounts for over half of all the region's putative central city expansion.)

Within these four regional groupings, there are significant differences among states. Texas cities account for 20 percent of all central city annexations in the nation, while California (9.8 percent), Oklahoma (9.2 percent), and Arizona (6.5 percent) have had many central cities involved in active annexation.

What accounts for such variations in annexation activity? One obvious explanation is differences in state laws regarding municipal annexation authority (Table 2.3). There would seem to have been some liberalization of annexation procedures over the past 40 years. Forty-four states now authorize municipal annexation; only Hawaii and five Northeastern states (Connecticut, Maine, New Hampshire, Rhode Island, and Vermont) do not have municipal annexation statutes, although two other Northeastern states (Massachusetts and Pennsylvania) have enacted such statutes just in the last 15 years.

More significant for differences in annexation activity are the various procedural hurdles that different state laws set up for successful annexation. Twelve of the 44 states that authorize annexation do not allow the city government itself to initiate annexation action by ordinance or resolution; in such states, annexation depends entirely on the initiative of property owners outside the city.

IT TOOK 40 YEARS, FROM IDEA TO COMPLETION, TO BUILD THE ORLEANS STREET VIADUCT. Although It Opened to Traffic on Jan. 3, 1936, Records of the Old Town Merchants Association, the Chief Boosters of the Project, Show That Plans for the ("Bath Street"!) Viaduct Had Been in the Making— and in Litigation—Since 1895.

Today, hundreds of cars an hour streak eastward and westward across the Orleans Street Viaduct. It's a boulevard from and to East and West Baltimore, eliminating the one-time need to snake back and forth through the ancient narrow streets that once led across the valley of the Jones Falls. But if you were around in the Baltimore of the 1920s and 1930s you would not have bet that the Orleans Street Viaduct would ever come into being.

To begin with, unlike so many civic projects, the viaduct was not the idea of the city planners. It was the child of commerce, conceived by the Old Town Merchants as a way to bring more customers into the then retail-rich Gay Street business complex. Over the years they made converts out of the city's traffic engineers.

First, there was the controversy surrounding *where* the viaduct should be built. Various proposals were hotly debated: minutes of the Old Town Association reveal early support for the bridge to be built from Old Town

(Gay and Orleans) to downtown along a line at about Hillen Street. Later, support swung to the present location, Gay Street to St. Paul at Franklin.

Then there was the even testier fight about what to call it. Over the years, at least four names were in contention: "Old Town Viaduct," "East West Viaduct," "Sky Line Viaduct," "Bath Street Viaduct." (The *Sun* editorialized in a pique, "Enter it in the archives as you will, it is still the Bath Street Viaduct, and that is what you had better ask to be directed to if you want to find it.")

But the biggest controversy was whether it should be built at all. When it was finally opened, news reports reflected on its stormy history: "The opening brought to a close one of the most intense legal controversies in the city's history."

Over the years litigation delayed progress, until Mayor Howard W. Jackson was pressed to revive the issue in the late 1920s. It would be 1934 before he would ceremoniously turn the
Continued on page 36

AFTER MASS
3-25-01

BORDERS®

BORDERS
Books * Music * Cafe
6151 Columbia Crossing
Columbia, MD 21045
410.290.0062

STORE: 0089   REG: 02/32   TRAN#: 6583
SALE   12/15/2000   EMP: 00106

BALTIMORE UNBOUND
                    ST T   15.95

          Subtotal   15.95
          MARYLAND 5%   .80
 1 Item Total   16.75
          VISA   16.75
ACCT # /S 4313033066063
               AUTH: 045950
NAME: BROOKS/THOMAS H

          CUSTOMER COPY

          12/15/2000 03:40PM

Thank you for shopping at Borders.
Try our Holiday Traditions coffee!

          Please visit our website @
          www.Borders.com

TABLE 2.3
State laws regarding municipal annexations (1993)

Number of States	South 16	West 13	Midwest 12	Northeast 9	Total 50
Municipal annexation authorized by state law	16	12	12	4	44
a. Initiated by property owner petition	12	10	9	3	34
b. Initiated by city ordinance or resolution	12	9	10	1	32
c. Public hearing required	10	8	7	2	27
d. Referendum and majority approval in city required	8	2	4	0	14
e. Referendum and/or majority approval in area to be annexed required	11	3	3	2	19
f. Approval of county governing authority required	1	6	4	0	11

Nineteen states require approval by referendum or petition by a majority of property owners in the area to be annexed; in many areas, such approval is more and more difficult to secure. Finally, the approval of the affected county government is required in 11 states—an increase of six since 1973. Where county government retains all its traditional county functions after annexation, county approval is often routine. However, where county governments increasingly provide urban services to new subdivisions—county services that would be supplanted by the municipality—county resistance can be strong.

An insurmountable barrier to central city expansion is the existence of other established municipalities around the city limits. Under state law, one municipality cannot annex property within another municipality. Some older cities, particularly in the Northeast and Midwest, have been substantially or completely hemmed in by smaller municipalities.

Finally, there is simply the question of the outlook and philosophy of local leadership. Throughout the Northeast and in parts of the Midwest, political geography is often viewed as immutable. There is little recognition that political jurisdictions ought to change and evolve dynamically with changing economic and demographic conditions. Many local leaders neither use the annexation opportunities they have nor press for changes in state statutes to provide more liberal authority.

IT TOOK **40** YEARS, FROM IDEA TO COMPLETION, TO BUILD THE ORLEANS STREET VIADUCT.
(continued)

first shovelful of dirt to officially begin the project.

The Grand Opening was scheduled for 6:45 p.m., December 31, 1935. Mayor Jackson was scheduled to join former Mayor William F. Broening (under whose administration the viaduct was first sponsored), along with Governor Harry W. Nice, Maryland's U.S. Senator George L. Radcliff, and dozens of VIP's to cut the ribbon. But it snowed all that day and the ceremony was postponed until January 6.

On January 6 it snowed all day again.

Before the city fathers could set another date, motorists got impatient with the whole Grand Opening business and worked their way around the barriers—putting the viaduct into use without a grand opening.

So the Orleans Street Viaduct was never "opened."

Given the long and tangled history of the project—it figures.

---

2. City-County Consolidation

City-county consolidation is a rare political event. Since World War II, there have been only 19 city-county consolidations. During the same period, voters have rejected such proposals over 100 times. Of the successful consolidations,

- five involved very small cities (Carson City, NV; Juneau, AK; Sitka, AK; Anaconda, MT; and Butte, MT);
- six were, in effect, defensive actions taken by suburban counties in Virginia's Tidewater area that "municipalized" to avoid further annexation by the City of Norfolk (e.g., Virginia Beach, Suffolk, and Chesapeake, VA); and
- only seven involved cities of sufficient size to be recognized as central cities (Anchorage, AK; Baton Rouge, LA; Nashville, TN; Jacksonville, FL; Indianapolis, IN; Columbus, GA; Lexington, KY; and Athens, GA).

Only 14 states have laws specifically authorizing city-county consolidation (see Table 2.4). However, few states have constitutional bars to such action. It is within the legal capabilities of most state legislatures to enact city-county consolidation statutes providing for whatever ground rules they choose—or to consolidate selected local governments outright by direct state statute.

Rare as city-county consolidations might be, they have accounted for 27 percent of all the geographic expansion of the 522 central cities (see Table 2.1). In practical terms, city-county consolidation is the maximum act of elasticity. Consolidations have had the most dramatic and positive effects on their communities. The following sections provide thumbnail descriptions of the three largest city-county consolidations.

A. Nashville–Davidson County

The consolidation of Nashville and Davidson County in 1962 turned around a declining central city and helped launch Nashville on the course of becoming *Music City, USA*. Before consolidation in 1962, Nashville had been a city of 22 square miles with 170,000 inhabitants. Its population had been dropping as residents deserted the city for new suburban subdivisions in Davidson County. Though Tennessee's state capital, downtown Nashville was decaying, and major businesses planned to move out.

Led by Davidson County Executive Beverly Brierly, consolidation by referendum created the "Metropolitan Government of Nashville–Davidson County" (Metro), an instant jurisdiction of over 400,000 people within 473 square miles. At the time of consolidation, however, six smaller municipalities, ranging in size from 1,500 to 5,500 residents, voted not to merge into Davidson County, so Nashville–Davidson still has six independent municipalities and seven special-purpose districts functioning within its borders.

TABLE 2.4
State laws regarding city-county consolidation (1993)

Number of States	South 16	West 13	Midwest 12	Northeast 9	Total 50
Authorized city-county consolidations	5	6	3	0	14
a. Referendum and majority approval of each city affected required	1	3	2	0	6
b. Referendum and majority approval of county required	4	3	0	0	7
c. Referendum and majority approval of unincorporated area of county required	0	0	1	0	1

Nashville–Davidson is governed by a mayor-council form of government. The mayor and vice-mayor are elected at-large, countywide, for four-year terms. The council is composed of the vice-mayor, who serves as chair, and 40 other members elected for four-year terms, 35 elected from single-member, equal-population districts and five elected at-large. The mayor is a "strong" mayor who serves as chief executive, appoints all senior administrative officials, prepares and submits the budget, and has veto power over council actions.

For service delivery and taxation purposes, Nashville–Davidson consists of two service/taxing districts. The General Services District (GSD) consists of the entire county and delivers services to all residents whether they are inside the consolidated jurisdiction or in the six independent municipalities. GSD services include parks and recreation, streets and roads, the sheriff's office, hospitals, and the airport as well as traditional county government functions (property value assessment, property tax collection, recording of deeds and other vital public records, etc.).

The Urban Services District (USD) delivers municipal-type services only within the participating urbanized portions of the county. USD services include police and fire protection, water supply, sanitary and storm sewers, street lighting and maintenance, and garbage collection.

Each of the two service districts has its own tax rate. Residents of the USD pay both USD and GSD property taxes, while those outside the USD pay only GSD property taxes. The USD may be expanded whenever the Metropolitan County Council determines that a given area needs urban services and Metro can supply such services within a year after USD taxes are levied on the area. In contrast to most other city-county consolidations, Nashville–Davidson assumed control over both the former city and former county school districts.

The six suburban municipalities that opted out of the consolidation may contract with Nashville–Davidson for the administration and handling of any of their governmental services. They are part of the GSD (that is, still part of Davidson County for traditional county functions), and their residents pay GSD property taxes. Nashville–Davidson is obligated to furnish them with the same level and quality of county services it makes available to the other portions of the GSD.

Among the positive impacts of consolidation have been more comprehensive areawide planning, problem solving, and program implementation; a more efficient collection and expenditure of local government funds attracting increased federal aid; pinpointing of administrative and political responsibility; decreases in city-suburban service disparities; and improved school and police services. While expanded and improved services resulted in tax increases in the former county portions of the consolidated government, voter surveys appeared to approve such increases as the trade-off for improved services.

Since consolidation, the Nashville metro area has been one of the nation's top economic performers. Between 1969 and 1989, real per capita income increased 49 percent for all metro area residents and 43 percent for Nashville–Davidson County residents. Over the 40-year period from 1950 to 1990 (the first decade of which Nashville and Davidson County were unconsolidated), Nashville's growth rate in real median family income was 176 percent (metro) and 161 percent (consolidated city). Among larger metro areas (i.e., 500,000 or more residents), Nashville–Davidson County's family income growth rate ranked sixth as a metro area and second as a central city.

Nashville–Davidson's economic success has supported steady regional population growth; the metro area is now an eight-county, 985,000-person region, the nation's 39th most populous. Its cost of living has remained below the national average (95 percent), having increased about 6 percent above the national rate of inflation during these decades of rapid development. Poverty levels are moderate (metro: 11.3 percent; city: 13.4 percent). Reflecting its broad jurisdictional coverage, Nashville–Davidson's fair share of poverty index is a low 119. On a neighborhood-by-neighborhood basis throughout the metro area, its residential segregation/integration index is 61; its high school integration index is 47. The strong fiscal health of city government is reflected in its AAA bond rating.

B. Jacksonville–Duval County

"Our consolidated government is the best form of local government in America," proclaimed Mayor Ed Austin at a community prayer breakfast October 1, 1993, celebrating the 25th anniversary of the consolidation of the City of Jacksonville and Duval County.

In an atmosphere of public crisis, in 1967, Jacksonville voters approved the consolidation by a 2–1 margin. Eight city officials had been indicted for corruption. All Duval County's high schools had lost their academic accreditation. Over 30,000 homes in county subdivisions depended on septic tanks, creating serious groundwater pollution. Dumping 600 million gallons of raw sewage per month into the St. John's River, the City of Jacksonville itself was the area's greatest polluter.

"A big part of the problem was the conflict and competition between city and county governments and agencies, and the fact that those governments duplicated each other's services, were laced with corruption, and spent money extravagantly," a commemorative publication noted 25 years later. "Most importantly, they lacked either the jurisdiction (the city) or the home rule powers (the county) necessary to cope with their problems."

At the time it was consolidated, the 769-square-mile Jacksonville became geographically the largest central city in the country. (In 1975, it was surpassed by 1,697-square-mile Anchorage, Alaska). Consolidation eliminated the five-member county commission and a unique and cumbersome double-headed city government in which executive power was vested in five elected city commissioners and legislative power was assigned to a separately elected nine-member council.

Under consolidation, executive power is vested in a strong mayor, elected at-large countywide, and legislative power is placed in a 19-member council, with 14 elected in single-member, equal-population districts, and five elected at-large, all for four-year terms. The mayor appoints the consolidated government's chief administrative officer and most department heads and has veto power over council actions. A number of separately elected officials have been retained (sheriff, civil service board, tax assessor, tax collector, and supervisor of elections). Independent authorities administer county hospitals, electricity supply, ports, public transportation, and downtown redevelopment. The planning commission and the school board are partially independent.

Jacksonville–Duval County is divided into a single, countywide General Services District (GSD) and five Urban Services Districts (USD), one each for Jacksonville and the four smaller municipalities that opted out of the consolidation (Baldwin and the Beaches). GSD services, delivered countywide, include fire and police protection, health, welfare, parks and recreation, public works (highways and roads), and housing and urban development. The USDs each deliver street lighting and cleaning, garbage and refuse collection, water supply, and sanitary sewers. The consolidated government provides such services for Jacksonville; the independent municipalities provide their own USD-type services.

Over its first quarter-century, Jacksonville has had a strong record of achievement to back up the current mayor's claim to excellence. In its first decade, the new government completed massive water/sewer and antipollution programs, including cleaning up the St. Johns River at a cost equivalent to $1.5 billion (in 1993 dollars). It installed 30,000 street lights and 2,000 fire hydrants and greatly upgraded the police, fire, and electric departments, while reducing taxes in 10 of its first 11 years.

Most impressive has been Jacksonville's economic performance. The government cites over $2 billion in new construction and 85,000 new jobs from some 160 companies recruited through the efforts of the local government and the Chamber of Commerce. Between 1969 and 1989, real incomes in metro Jacksonville grew 50 percent, one of the highest rates in the nation. From 1950 to 1990 (half of that period as a consolidated government), Jacksonville's growth in real median family income was 145 percent (metro) and 143 percent (city).

Despite rapid growth, Jacksonville's cost of living has been stable and remains below the national metro average (95 percent). Though it is in historically poor North Florida, its poverty rate is modest (metro: 11.8 percent; city: 13.0 percent), and with a broad jurisdictional base like Nashville–Davidson, its city fair share of poverty index is a near-parity 110. In terms of black residential segregation/integration, its metro-wide index is 58, while, with only four countywide school systems, classroom integration measures 47. Though the economy is strong, past overcommitments on bond issues have kept Jacksonville's bond rating at a modest A1.

Assessing his community's economic vigor, Hans Tanzler, who served as mayor for the new government's first decade, explained, "the dream of businessmen is to have a 'one-stop' local government, where they could come to one place which had all the authority and resources to solve their problems. Well, that dream exists, I would tell them, and it is here in Jacksonville."

C. Indianapolis–Marion County

The largest postwar city-county consolidation occurred in 1969 and united the City of Indianapolis and Marion County into a new "Unigov" government. It is the only modern city-county consolidation to be effected without voter approval, having been accomplished by statute enacted by the Indiana state legislature.

Such a unique political event implies a unique set of circumstances—and by 1969, Indianapolis' circumstances were certainly unique. On January 1, 1968, 35-year-old Richard Lugar became the first Republican mayor of Indianapolis in 16 years (and only the third Republican mayor in 40 years). When Republicans scored heavy victories statewide in November 1968, Mayor Lugar realized that the political stars were aligned just right for a dramatic initiative. For the first time this century, Republicans had elected the mayor, a strong majority of the Indianapolis City Council, all of the Marion County Commissioners, all members of the county legislative delegation, strong majorities in both houses of the State General Assembly, and a Republican governor.

Though there was a long-standing interest in consolidation among business and civic groups, Mayor Lugar had two overall goals in driving consolidation through the Republican-controlled political system. The first goal was to create a more effective and efficient structure of local governance; above all, Lugar sought to strengthen the mayor's office as the preeminent areawide leadership post. The second goal was to broaden the city government's electoral base to absorb Republican-voting suburban areas outside the city limits; having won the mayor's office, Lugar proposed to lock it up for the Republican Party for decades to come through city-county consolidation. With hard lobbying and astute compromises, Lugar succeeded brilliantly. Both his community and partisan goals have been thoroughly fulfilled.

At the time of consolidation, Marion County had a population of 794,000 with Indianapolis, its dominant city and the Indiana state capital, having 525,000 or nearly 70 percent of its total population. Of Marion County's 396 square miles, Indianapolis occupied 82 square miles. The county contained only three other municipalities of over 10,000 population and none over 20,000.

Unigov took effect on January 1, 1970. It is governed by a major-council form of government. The mayor is chief executive of the combined Indianapolis–Marion County and is elected at-large every four years. The mayor is "strong," having charge of six of Unigov's departments: administration, metropolitan development, public works, transportation, public safety, and parks and recreation. But a number of countywide functions remain outside the mayor's administrative control, including public education, welfare, the libraries, and the airport, all of which are governed by independent special districts, only a few of which are subject to Unigov budgetary controls. The city/county council consists of 29 members—25 elected by district and four elected at-large—all for four year terms. Although consolidated with Indianapolis into Unigov, Marion County still retains a number of independent, separately elected functional officials: assessor, auditor, treasurer, sheriff, prosecutor, coroner, recorder, and surveyor. Unigov does not include three municipalities and nine townships remaining in Marion County, nor 11 separate school districts and a number of other special districts.

Providing vigorous community leadership as well as administering more effective public services was the primary goal of Mayor Lugar's vision. Lugar and his successors, William Hudnut and Steven Goldsmith, have clearly provided that leadership.

A dozen years after Unigov began, *The Wall Street Journal* commented that

> Indianapolis has done something that few of its putatively more cosmopolitan Northern neighbors can match: it has held its own against the Sun Belt in the war for population and jobs. It has even gained a bit.

The article attributed the Republican mayors' special success to their ability to interest the Indianapolis business community in Unigov's development plans and also noted,

> One big reason Indianapolis has been able to do what it has in the last dozen years is the unusual Unigov system, the partial consolidation of city and Marion County government that took effect in 1970.

A history of Unigov concluded that

> Unigov created a structure that focused real authority in the mayor's office to provide for more efficient government. In addition, Unigov also helped inspire a sense of community accomplishment that has helped coalesce private-sector leadership. . . . It is impossible to say with any precision which of the elements is the more effective in promoting the synergistic and mutually beneficial private-public leadership that has emerged. Certainly, however, Unigov provided the necessary focus for the community to rally around in removing its long-enduring "Indian-No-Place" image.

Indianapolis has weathered the economic storms better than almost any other Midwestern industrial community. From 1950 to 1990 (half those years under Unigov), real median family income rose 115 percent (metro) and 95 percent (city). Over the last two decades (since Unigov), real per capita incomes rose 32 percent (metro) and 24 percent (city).

Over the four decades, the relative cost of living has declined 4 percent to 94 percent. Like other consolidated communities, Indianapolis' fair share of poverty index is a not very burdensome 130 (metro: 9.6 percent; city: 12.5 percent,—which should be further adjusted downward for the low cost of living.) By the dissimilarity index, the Indianapolis area has a disappointingly high level of racial segregation (educational: 62; residential: 74). In part that is a function of the almost totally white character of the seven counties surrounding Indianapolis–Marion County. All progress in racial integration has occurred totally within

Unigov's jurisdiction. Unigov's bond rating is strictly blue-chip (AAA).

• • •

In summary, the three city-county consolidated governments cited as examples are all moving into the 21st century as successful core communities at the heart of vigorously competitive regions. Economic growth rates are high, and costs of living are below average. Poverty levels regionwide are modest, and the central cities are not unduly burdened by little more than their fair share of the region's poor. Though much still must be achieved in terms of promoting racial justice, these communities at least are less segregated than their competitors (which is about the best that can be said for any American community).

TWO-TIER SYSTEMS OF LOCAL GOVERNMENT

1. Empowered Urban Counties

For over half of the nation's 320 metro areas, a potential framework for metropolitan government is already in place. That framework is county government. In 1990, over half of the country's metro areas (165) were defined as single-county metro areas. The majority of single-county metro areas are relatively small; 94 percent have fewer than 200,000 residents. Single-county metro areas, however, do include some of the country's largest population centers, such as Florida's Broward County (1.3 million residents: Ft. Lauderdale–Hollywood–Pompano Beach) and Dade County (1.9 million: Miami–Hialeah–Miami Beach); Arizona's Maricopa County (2.1 million: Phoenix); and California's Santa Clara County (1.4 million: San Jose), Orange County (2.4 million: Anaheim–Santa Ana), San Diego County (2.5 million), and Los Angeles County (8.8 million). Outside these Sunbelt giants, there are also some large, single-county metro areas in the Frostbelt, such as New York's Erie County (968,532: Buffalo) and Washington's Pierce County (586,203: Tacoma).

In practical terms, 100 percent of a metro area need not be under one local government jurisdiction to approximate the benefits of more unified governance. Having 60 percent or more of the area under a unified government would probably be sufficient. By this more liberal standard, single-county jurisdictions embrace 60 percent or more of a metro area's population in 256 of 320 metro areas (80 percent), containing 104 million people (or 55 percent of the country's metro population). Indeed, in 22 of the 42 metro areas of more than one million residents, the principal county covers 60 percent or more of the metro population.

Thus, county governments are ready-made vehicles for serving as metro or quasi-metro governments. Indeed, many urban counties have become major deliverers of services, particularly in the fields of health and welfare. Only in New England states, such as Connecticut (which abolished counties in 1959) and Massachusetts (where counties are little more than state judicial districts), would a county-oriented strategy for achieving greater unity of metro governance require building new governmental institutions almost from scratch.

In terms of diminishing racial and economic segregation, the key powers that county government must exercise are land use, planning, and zoning; assisted housing for low-income groups; and equitable financing of public services. To be meaningful, these powers must be exercised without being subject to veto by municipalities within the county.

There are county governments that exercise such powers, such as Montgomery County and Prince George's County, Maryland, and Fairfax County, Virginia, in the Washington, D.C.–Maryland–Virginia metro area. However, in no large metro area does a fully empowered county currently dominate the metro area's development policies to the extent of King County in the Seattle, Washington metro area.

A. King County, Washington

The two-county Seattle metro area's population is 1,972,961, of which, with a population of 1,507,319, King County represents 76 percent. (Snohomish County accounts for the remainder.) Even when combined with the Tacoma metro area, the Seattle-Tacoma Consolidated Metropolitan Statistical Area, King County represents 59 percent of the area's population. Some 2,200 square miles, King County is the 13th most populous county in America.

King County's emergence as a potential metro government resulted from two recent developments: its absorption of Metro, a special transit and water district, in January 1994 and new planning powers conferred on King County under the State of Washington's new Growth Management Act.

1) Consolidation of Seattle Metro   On November 3, 1992, the voters of King County approved the consolidation of Metro into

King County government. This vote marked the opening of a new chapter in the effort of Seattle area residents to develop effective metro governance.

Metro was created in response to a growing environmental crisis 30 years ago. Rapid postwar suburbanization of the Seattle area had led to untreated wastes polluting Lake Washington. The 29 incorporated cities and towns, unincorporated subdivisions, and a King County government that was viewed as backward, ineffective, even corrupt, seemed incapable of devising a common solution.

In 1957, the state legislature passed enabling legislation to allow, upon local voter approval, organization of a "metropolitan municipal corporation." The King County–wide municipality would not replace any local governments but would sit functionally above the City of Seattle and the other 28 municipalities. The legislature empowered such a supramunicipality to provide certain municipal-type services: water pollution abatement, public transportation, comprehensive planning, water supply, garbage disposal, and parks administration.

In 1958, the Seattle and King County voters activated this "Municipality of Metropolitan Seattle." However, the voters initially empowered Metro to deal only with the water pollution problem. In 1973, they voted Metro additional authority to operate a mass transit system within King County.

For more than 30 years, Metro was governed by a federated Metro Council composed of the elected leadership of constituent governments. The Metro Council ultimately included the mayor and all nine members of the Seattle City Council, the King County executive and all nine members of the King County Council, representatives of all other cities with more than 15,000 population (cities of over 50,000 population were entitled to an additional seat for each increment of 15,000 residents), one representative of the smaller cities, six members appointed by the Metro Council itself from each of the six County Council districts, and a commissioner from the Metro sewer district. By 1992, with the growth of the region's population, the Metro Council had grown from its original 16 members to 45 members.

By 1992, Metro had evolved into a major, well-respected, countywide special-purpose district. It had succeeded so well in its original mission—to clean up Lake Washington—that in 1960, Metro became the first noncity to win national "All-American City" recognition. Setting ridership records, in 1992 the 4,000-employee Metro was also named best transit agency in the nation by the American Public Transit Association.

However, controversy increasingly revolved around the makeup and power of the federated Metro Council. After a failed effort in 1979 to merge Metro with King County government and a dozen abortive measures to reorganize the Metro Council by the state legislature, the debate over Metro took a decisive turn in 1990 when a federal District judge ruled that the Metro Council's federated structure violated the constitutional one-person, one-vote guarantee.

After three years of local controversy, legislative debate, and missed court deadlines, the various city and county officials on the Metro Council decided to propose merging Metro and King County. Their intent was to improve regional growth management and environmental protection by unifying services and powers that were divided between the two governments.

Their plan acknowledged a major transformation within King County government since the original founding of Metro. In 1968, voters had adopted a "home rule" charter for King County. The three-member Board of County Commissioners was replaced by a nine-member County Council and an elected County Executive. Over the next 25 years, King County had matured into a competent, professional urban county government.

Under the merger proposal approved by the voters in November 1992, a single legislative body—the Metropolitan County Council—replaced the King County and Metro Councils, in effect expanding the King County Council from 9 to 13 members elected by district. To give cities "a voice and a vote" in developing countywide comprehensive planning policies, three new bodies were mandated in a charter amendment to the King County charter:

1. a Regional Transit Committee to address transit policies, fiscal policies, long-range capital improvement planning, capital facilities siting policies, and service design and subsidy allocation policies;

2. a Regional Water Quality Committee to deal with regional water quality plans, fiscal policies (including rate structure), long-range capital plans, facilities siting, and extension policies; and

3. a Regional Policy Committee to address public health, human services, jail, and other criminal justice services, placement of regional facilities, and other issues as appropriate.

Each committee has 12 voting members—six Metro County Council members and six members divided between Seattle and suburban cities. (In the case of the Water Quality Committee, there

THE SUBWAY FINALLY BEGAN OPERATION IN 1982.
But Plans to Build It Go Back as Far as 1920!
"Mt. Washington to St. Paul and Franklin."

Layton Smith was a prophet without honor in his own country—a poet of sorts, a city planner out of his time. His time was the 1920s—and his dream was an underground rapid transit system for Baltimore. His subway system (presented to the city at the Engineers Club on the evening of June 8, 1920) would begin in Mt. Washington at Falls Road and roll under Falls Road to Cold Spring Lane and then east to Roland Avenue, then south to University Parkway and Charles Street, then to North Avenue, to Cathedral Street, still underground to St. Paul and Franklin. Here it would come into what Smith called the "Grand Central Exchange." In the Exchange one could: (a) stay aboard to proceed underground to St. Paul and Center Street and there to Hanover Street all the way down (and under) Hanover until the train surfaced to cross the Hanover Street bridge to Curtis Bay or (b) board the train east to Highlandtown or (c) board it west all the way out Park Heights Avenue. There is no record of how Smith's subway plan was received, but we can imagine the deafening silence that greeted his grandiose plans, and we know that not a shovelful of earth was turned to start a subway system until 1977.

Given the long and torturous history of the subway and Mr. Smith's unsung status, Mr. Smith ought to be honored, and it's not too late. A subway car ought to be named "The Layton F. Smith," and when it whooshes to a stop on the day of its naming and the applause breaks out and the movers and shakers are flush with success, someone should propose a modest toast: "To Layton F. Smith, who first dreamed the dream."

It only took Baltimore 63 years to fulfill it!

---

are only four municipal members and two members from independent water districts.) The Metro County Council is the only body that is legally empowered to enact plans and policies; however, it can override a regional committee recommendation only if at least eight of the 13 council members agree. Otherwise, a regional committee's recommendations automatically become law.

2) Washington's Growth Management Act   Within this new structure, the Metropolitan County Council is undertaking new responsibilities to implement the State of Washington's Growth Management Act of 1990. Under the new state law, the Metro County Council is ultimately responsible for developing a long-range development plan for King County. The plan must adopt an Urban Growth Boundary. In developing the plan, the Metropolitan County Council must engage in a complex process of consultation and negotiation with the county's 34 municipalities (including the City of Seattle). Ultimately, the Metropolitan County Council will adopt the areawide plan, to whose provisions all municipal governments must conform. The areawide plan includes goals and policies to promote fair share affordable housing.

In 1993, the County Council rejected a proposed 2,200-acre, 4,500-unit new community in eastern King County called Grand Ridge. Viewed as an unprecedented action in the history of the region's development, the rejection of Grand Ridge was interpreted locally as a strong affirmation of King County's commitment to prevent suburban sprawl beyond the projected Urban Growth Boundary. The County Council's action was also seen as boosting Seattle Mayor Norman Rice's strategy of revitalizing Seattle's declining neighborhoods as "urban villages."

A recent King County publication sums up the outlook for the future:

> For the past 50 years, in attempting to respond to [regional] issues, King County citizens were burdened with a fractured regional government system that often lacked the necessary tools and sufficient accountability. On January 1, 1994 that [changed] as citizens [took] possession of a unified Metro-King County government with the potential to more effectively deal with regional problems.

2. Metropolitan Governments

While there are literally hundreds of intergovernmental structures of metropolitan scope, in reality, there are practically no true metropolitan governments. The National Association of Regional Councils lists 669 councils of government, regional planning councils, and areawide economic development districts among its current (or prospective) members, yet almost none has any authority over such crucial issues as land use planning and zoning policies— that is, public policies shaping where different groups of people live. What political clout regional councils have often derives from delegation of limited powers over federal aid for local governments. Many regional councils came into being as mechanisms for local review and comment on federal grant-in-aid projects (the so-called "A-95 review process," which was repealed under President Reagan in 1982). More recently, new life has been breathed into regional councils by the federal Clean Air Act amendments of 1989 and the federal Intermodal Surface Transportation Efficiency Act of 1991. Under the latter act, in particular, regional councils have broad authority to allocate and approve over $10 billion annually in federal highway and transit projects.

However, such regional bodies are either voluntary councils of local elected officials or specialized organizations (such as economic development districts) without the broad authority of local units of general government. Such voluntary organizations, in the judgment of the National Civic League, are unable

> to address the difficult problems [because] elected officials either lack the courage or the will to address them, for example, fair share housing, comprehensive regional land use and transportation planning, revenue base sharing, and tax increases. . . . Voluntary councils of government have assiduously avoided policies and arrangements which would result in sharing the social burdens of inner city populations or otherwise breaching the social insulation of the suburbs from their central city problems.

Against this background, the evolution of the Portland, Oregon Metropolitan Services District ("Metro") is of great significance as a model for other regions.

A. Portland's "Metro"

> We, the people of the Portland area metropolitan services district, in order to establish an elected, visible and accountable regional government that is responsive to the citizens of the region and works cooperatively with our local governments; that undertakes, as its most important services, planning and policy making to preserve and enhance the quality of life and the environment for ourselves and future generations; and that provides regional services needed and desired by the citizens in an efficient and effective manner, do ordain this charter for the Portland area metropolitan services district, to be known as "Metro."

With that preamble, Portland area voters adopted November 3, 1992, a "home rule" charter for the Portland Metropolitan Services District. On the same election day that, 200 miles north, Seattle area voters were merging a limited-powers "Metro" into King County government, Portland area voters were expanding the powers of their regional government.

For almost 70 years, the Portland area—now three counties and 24 municipalities—has been experimenting with various forms of metro cooperation. As early as 1925, a state study commission was concerned that the impact of the automobile was allowing rapid and unplanned suburbanization to outrun both the provision of urban services and the pace of annexation to Portland. It recommended new legislation to facilitate the consolidation of Portland and Multnomah County—a proposal that the Oregon legislature studiously ignored.

The postwar boom revived concern with unplanned regional growth. During the 1950s, Multnomah, Clackamas, and Washington Counties all adopted their first zoning codes. In response to federal aid requirements, two research and planning organizations—the Metropolitan Planning Commission (1957–1966) and the Portland-Vancouver Metropolitan Transportation Study (1959–1967)—came into existence. They sought to bring some order to the area's burgeoning growth. On the services front, by 1961 the number of special districts for fire, water, zoning, sewers, parks, and lighting had exploded to 218 (from 28 in 1941). On the political front, a war was raging over aggressive annexation efforts by Portland, countered by suburban communities' struggle to incorporate as a defense against annexation.

However, these two bodies were essentially research organizations without substantive powers. To achieve more substantive regional institutions, the League of Women Voters, business leaders, and other "good government" groups encouraged the legislature to establish the Portland Metropolitan Study Commission (1963–1971). PMSC's recommendations ultimately transformed regional governance. PMSC helped to organize the Columbia Region Association of Governments (CRAG) in 1967, then succeeded in gaining legislative approval for the Portland Metropolitan Area Local Government Boundary Commission (1969) and the Metropolitan Service District (1970)— the birth of Metro.

The Metropolitan Services District (MSD) was conceived as a flexible governmental "box" into which the voters of its three county jurisdictions or the legislature could assign service responsibilities that they selected. It began life uncertainly and modestly. Over the implacable opposition of Portland city officials, the MSD was activated by referendum on May 26, 1970, by a 54 percent to 46 percent margin. It was governed by a seven-member, federated board of local elected officials—one each from Portland and the three counties, three representing other cities in each of the counties. Denied a general property tax base by another voter referendum, its first project—planning a regional solid waste disposal system—was financed by a small tax on used auto tires. In 1976, MSD added a second regional function—operating the Washington Park Zoo—with the city of

Portland's agreement and voter approval of an earmarked tax levy.

During these years, CRAG was embroiled in increasing frustration and controversy. As its membership grew from the original four counties and 14 cities to five counties and 31 cities, CRAG had neither the authority nor the ability to forge a consensus around difficult regional policy issues.

> The difficulty in building consensus around a [comprehensive regional land use plan] reflected a fundamental tension in using the council of governments model to develop regional policies. . . . [CRAG board members] were often torn between the imperatives of regional issues and the need to protect their own community from unwanted costs, programs, or development initiatives.

By 1977, acting on the recommendations of a citizen-based Tri-County Commission, the legislature gave MSD its own directly elected 12 member board, an elected chief executive, local taxing authority (but only by voter referendum), and CRAG's regional planning responsibilities. (In the process, the legislature abolished CRAG.) Direct election of the MSD board members was supported as "the best, and perhaps only, way to secure a democratic, responsive, responsible and effective area-wide government." Direct election of the MSD's executive officer also followed the Tri-County Commission's view that "a hired chief administrator, lacking both a political base and a direct line of accountability to the citizens, simply could not survive in a unit the size of the revised MSD." In May 1978, the voters of the three-county area approved the revised MSD by a 55 percent to 45 percent margin.

Despite early setbacks (two more tax referenda went down to defeat), MSD slowly grew in further responsibility and reputation. In 1979, the Oregon Land Conservation and Development Commission accepted the Portland area Urban Growth Boundary drawn up by MSD. The Washington Park Zoo grew in attendance and national recognition. Buttressed by an advisory council of local officials, MSD took over planning the use of federal transportation funds. In 1986, voters in the three-county area approved a $65 million bond issue for the Oregon Convention Center to be planned, constructed, and operated by MSD (through a subsidiary organization).

In 1987, the legislature provided the MSD's chief executive with veto power over Council actions while the MSD Council itself moved more into an independent, legislative mode of operation. The legislature also strengthened MSD by shifting appointment of the Boundary Commission members from the Governor to the MSD chief executive (from nominations submitted by MSD councillors). Finally, in 1990, the Oregon constitution was amended to allow MSD to have its own home rule charter. Drawn up by the Metro Home Rule Charter Committee, it was this document that voters approved in November 1992.

The structural changes provided in Metro's home rule charter are minimal. Council membership is reduced from 12 members to 7. The smaller council provides policy direction to the work of the now $225 million-a-year agency with 1,200 employees, who are supervised by Metro's elected chief executive.

However, most critical for the Portland area's future are new initiatives in the planning and growth management of regional land use. In recent years, the MSD adopted an ambitious set of "Regional Urban Growth Goals and Objectives" to guide local government land use, transportation, housing, and economic development planning. That function received a resounding endorsement from the area's citizenry, who affirmed in the new charter that regional planning is Metro's "primary function."

The charter charged Metro with developing a 50-year "Future Vision" ("Portland 2040") and a "Regional Framework Plan" by December 1997. The charter then empowered the Metro Council to adopt ordinances that require local comprehensive plans and zoning regulations to comply with the Regional Framework Plan. Metro will adjudicate inconsistencies between regional and local plans and can change inconsistent local land use standards and procedures.

After extensive public discussion of four alternative growth concepts, the Metro Council adopted a plan in December 1994, expanding modestly the Urban Growth Boundary. The Regional Framework Plan will be adopted in December 1995.

After decades of patient development, the Portland Metro represents a powerful but flexible structure for addressing many of the region's most critical problems.

B. Metro Toronto

The most powerful, best-established, and best-known metropolitan government in North America belongs to the same community as the winners of the 1993 championship of America's national pastime (baseball)—Toronto, Canada.

The history of Metro Toronto also illustrates three themes that pervade the history of metropolitan development in the United States:

1. the continuous outward expansion of urbanization (despite efforts at controlling growth),
2. the critical role played by Canadian provincial governments in forging metropolitan policies and institutions (by contrast with the generally indifferent record of state governments in the United States); and
3. the jealousy with which local governments protect their powers (in the face of strong metropolitan structures backed by the authority of provincial government).

1) The Evolution of Metro Toronto   From its founding as the Town of York, capital of the Province of Upper Canada, in 1793, the City of Toronto has always dominated its region. Incorporated as the City of Toronto in 1834, the city expanded in population and area through immigration and annexation. Annexation virtually ceased by the 1920s, as new suburban municipalities began to resist further annexation by the city. Nevertheless, by 1941, the City of Toronto's population (655,752) was still nearly three-quarters of the metropolitan area population (892,179).

In the postwar period, however, in metro Toronto as in U.S. metro areas, suburban expansion accelerated. Suburban towns were under heavy fiscal pressure to provide basic infrastructure, while concerns were rising about uncoordinated development. By 1952, the solution of Toronto city officials was to press for a "unitary" government. As a result, the city formally applied to the Ontario Municipal Board to expand Toronto by "amalgamating" Toronto with all 11 neighboring municipalities within the traditional Metropolitan Area of Toronto. The city's proposal was vigorously opposed by all but one of the 11 suburban municipalities.

In January 1953, the Ontario Municipal Board (a provincial government commission deciding annexation disputes) rejected the City of Toronto's petition for amalgamation but proposed to replace it with a two-tier federated government. In February 1953, the prime minister of Ontario introduced Bill 80, "An Act to Provide for the Federation of the Municipalities in the Metropolitan Area," into the provincial parliament. (Under the Canadian constitution, the provinces have total responsibility for local government affairs.) The proposal was enacted readily under the principle of party discipline in Parliament.

In January 1954, the new Municipality of Metropolitan Toronto (Metro Toronto) took effect. It was governed by a Metropolitan Council of 25 appointed representatives—12 elected officials selected by the City of Toronto; the mayor, or "reeve," from each of the now 12 suburban municipalities; and a chairman, Frederick G. Gardiner, appointed by the Prime Minister of Ontario. (Gardiner was subsequently elected to serve two terms as chairman until his retirement in 1961.) A Metropolitan School Board was also established with the same pattern of representation from local school boards. Toronto's representation reflected its 50 percent share of the area's population at the time.

The metro government assumed certain functions (primarily infrastructure development) while the existing 13 municipalities continued to provide a wide variety of services.

Metro Toronto was charged with:

1. water supply—constructing and maintaining pumping stations, treatment plants, trunk mains, and reservoirs for the wholesale distribution of water to the 13 "Area Municipalities" (including the city);
2. sewage disposal—constructing and maintaining trunk sewage mains and treatment plants capable of handling sewage from all 13 Area Municipalities;
3. roads—establishing an arterial system of highways (with financing split with the provincial government);
4. public transit—through the Toronto Transit Commission, operating all bus and subway services through the metro area;
5. education—giving the Metropolitan School Board responsibility for coordinating educational facilities and providing financial grants to local school boards;
6. health and welfare—providing homes for the aged, wards for the Children's Aid Societies, post-sanitorium care for tuberculosis patients, and hospitalization for indigent patients;
7. criminal justice—maintaining a courthouse and jail;
8. housing—giving Metropolitan Council all the powers of a municipality in the fields of housing and redevelopment. (In practical effect, no overall housing role was initially provided at metro level, since this authorization merely placed Metro Toronto on a par with all the constituent municipalities.);
9. planning—creating the Metropolitan Planning Board, whose authority extended beyond the metropolitan area, encompassing all adjoining townships. It was charged with preparing an official plan for this larger metropolitan plan-

ning area for future approval by the provincial government;

10. parks—establishing metropolitan (i.e., regional) parks; and

11. finance and taxation—being responsible for uniform assessment of all lands and buildings in the 13 Area Municipalities. On the basis of total assessment, the fiscal needs
of the Metropolitan Council were levied against each Area
Municipality at a uniform mill rate. Each Area Municipality then collected the metropolitan tax requirement, as
well as its own revenues, from local taxpayers. The Metropolitan Council was given sole power of issuing bonded
indebtedness both for itself and for Area Municipalities
and also assumed all outstanding school bonds. The Metropolitan Council acquired all assets of Area Municipalities necessary for its metropolitan services.

The following functions were retained by the Area Municipalities:

1. water supply—providing local distribution and retail sales;

2. sewage disposal—constructing and maintaining local sewers;

3. garbage collection—collecting all local garbage;

4. roads—constructing and maintaining local streets and
sidewalks;

5. police—providing all police services (by the late 1970s, all
police services had been unified into a Metropolitan Police Department);

6. fire—providing all fire prevention and fire suppression services;

7. education—allowing local boards of education to continue
and to finance the cost of any standard of educational service above the level supported by the metropolitan grants;

8. health and welfare—providing all public health services,
unemployment relief, and social work services;

9. housing—retaining all their powers in housing and redevelopment through their local councils;

10. planning—planning through local boards *in conformity
with the overall metropolitan plan* (emphasis added);

11. parks—constructing and maintaining local parks; and

12. finance and taxation—on the basis of the Metropolitan
Council–established uniform assessment, collecting all
local revenues required for local services (as well as collecting the Metropolitan Council's revenues).

Over the next two decades, Metro Toronto largely concentrated on meeting the infrastructure needs of a rapidly growing area. It used the economic power and property tax base of the City of Toronto to finance suburban infrastructure. The populations of the 12 suburban municipalities continued to grow (as did their own tax resources).

By the mid-1960s, criticism was growing of the lower proportional representation of the increasingly populous suburban towns within the Metropolitan Council. Therefore, in 1966, the provincial government acted again, reorganizing the City of Toronto and the 12 suburban municipalities into "one city and five boroughs." The City of Toronto was expanded slightly to incorporate the Villages of Swansea and Forest Hill. The remaining ten municipalities were consolidated around the largest to create the Boroughs of East York, Etobicoke, North York, Scarborough, and York. The City of Toronto retained its 12 seats on the Metropolitan Council, but the Council was expanded from 25 to 33 members (including the chairman) to accommodate additional representation for the growing boroughs. In short, though the City of Toronto remained the principal employment center and tax base for Metro Toronto, because of its slowly declining population within Metro Toronto, its representation on the Metro Council fell from one-half to almost one-third.

Until 1971, most regional population growth continued within the boundaries of Metropolitan Toronto (though the City of Toronto itself slowly lost population). In the last two decades, urbanization has been reaching out beyond Metro Toronto's 240-square-mile area into a much larger region of 2,700 square miles now designated as the Greater Toronto Area.

In 1969, Frederick Gardiner published two farewell articles, entitled "Metro Must Expand or Be Strangled" and "An Iron Curtain Must Not Stifle Metro." In these articles, Metro Toronto's first chairman argued:

> Right now, Metro has an unlimited potential for future development into one of the most important cities on the continent. If Metro is surrounded by an iron curtain of municipalities preventing its natural growth, the development of the whole area would be thwarted.
>
> The main difficulty at the moment is that practically all of the land in Metropolitan Toronto is developed. Future development must either be on land which is far beyond an economical cost or the development must be a vertical one with multi-story buildings for residential purposes. In the case of industry it will go where single-story buildings can be built at an economical cost.

"Metro should be allowed to expand naturally without artificial boundaries," Gardiner urged. He concluded by recommending that Metro's boundaries be formally expanded to about 700 square miles. The older Boroughs of East York and York would be incorporated into the City of Toronto; two very large, semirural areas to the north (Vaughan and Markham) would be added; and Pickering Township to the east of Metro would be added as a seventh borough.

Neither then nor in the quarter-century since has the Province of Ontario responded to Gardiner's plea. Instead, Metro Toronto's jurisdiction has remained its original 240-square-mile area, while the provincial government has created two-tier local governments for the newer urbanizing areas. The regional governments of Durham (eight towns), Halton (four towns), Peel (three towns), and York (ten towns—not to be confused with York Borough within Metro Toronto) now carry out Metro-type responsibilities within their respective regions. A variety of provincial ministries try to provide overall policy direction and coordination of services for the Greater Toronto Area.

The latest reform was instituted in 1988 when the provincial parliament abandoned the federated nature of the Metropolitan Council—that is, a council composed of elected officials of member governments. It established direct, popular election of council members from 34 wards that cover Metropolitan Toronto. Under the "one person, one vote" principle, the City of Toronto's representation has fallen to nine of 34 members—barely one-quarter of the Council. Nevertheless, members from the City of Toronto continue to be influential, since, on the basis of its tax base, the City of Toronto provides over 40 percent of the Metropolitan Council's revenues.

Assessing the history of Metropolitan Toronto, a Canadian scholar has written,

> The development of Metropolitan Toronto has been characterized by the maintenance of a strong central city; higher suburban densities than are found in most North American metropolitan areas; a diversity of land uses in all area municipalities; *the dispersal of publicly assisted, low income housing throughout the suburbs* [emphasis added]; and a transportation system in which public transit (subways, light rapid transit, and an extensive bus network) has played a prominent role.

Beyond the contribution made by metropolitan planning, the author cites as other important factors:

> 1. the incentive given Metro's suburban members to support measures of benefit to the central city by . . . basing contributions to Metro on assessment rather than population;

2. the relatively large size of [Metro's] five suburbs (particularly the outer suburbs of Etobicoke, North York, and Scarborough), which enhanced their ability to accommodate a large variety of residential and employment activities;

3. suburban enthusiasm . . . for high-density residential buildings, which were perceived to yield more in revenues than they cost to serve;

4. provincial regulations [regarding] strict environmental controls . . . which meant that the outward spread of development would keep pace with the outward extension of [Lake Ontario]-oriented sewer and water services;

5. *a strong provincial role in the provision of publicly assisted family housing* [emphasis added]; and

6. the success of Metro's first subway, opened the year Metro began, . . . [which] undoubtedly contributed to the continuing economic strength of the core city.

Though not without its flaws and shortcomings, Metro Toronto has been vital in bringing to the Greater Toronto Area the balance and social stability absent in so many American metro areas. The end result is, by common consent, North America's most livable major metropolitan area.

REQUIRING LOCAL GOVERNMENTS TO SHARE REGIONAL RESPONSIBILITIES

1. Affordable Housing

A. *Connecticut*

1) The Affordable Housing Appeals Process   Connecticut is the country's wealthiest state (at least, in nominal per capita income). In sad contrast, its metro areas also rank ninth in racial segregation and first in economic segregation.

Such racial and economic disparities are a product of Connecticut's housing patterns and system of local governance. Central cities are dominated by rental properties. (Eighty percent of Hartford's residents are renters.) Suburban towns are overwhelmingly oriented toward owner-occupied homes—at towering prices. In 1990, median home costs ranged from a low of $140,000 (Bridgeport) to over $500,000 (half a dozen towns including Greenwich and Stamford).

Beyond the issue of social segregation, such high housing costs exacted a high political and emotional price. First, many Connecticut public employees (police officers, firefighters, teachers) cannot afford to live in the communities they serve. Second, as one legislator summarized, "Our children cannot afford to live in the communities where they grew up."

In response, the Connecticut General Assembly has enacted a sustained package of initiatives to stimulate more affordable housing. A central problem, in the eyes of many reformers, is the belief that many Connecticut towns kept low- and moderate-income families out of their communities through exclusionary zoning, that is, by adopting land use practices such as large lots, minimum house sizes, and bans on multifamily housing that raised housing costs. Town governments countered that these measures protected public health and safety—a defense to which the state courts have traditionally deferred.

To counter exclusionary zoning, the legislature explicitly directed towns to adopt "inclusionary zoning" practices. This included density bonuses, which allow developers to build more housing units per acre than local zoning would normally permit if they also build some affordable units.

To put enforcement teeth behind this policy, the Connecticut General Assembly has enacted the Affordable Housing Land Use Appeals Procedure (Public Act 89-311). Under the new procedure, if a town rejects a developer's affordable housing proposal, the developer can challenge the local ruling in state court. The burden of proof rests with the town to prove that its reasons for rejecting the project would "clearly outweigh the need for affordable housing." In effect, the legislature has defined the state's need for affordable housing as the primary public interest and has shifted the burden of proof from developers to town planning commissions.

Though suits can originate from communities throughout the state, appeals are heard only by the State Superior Court in Hartford–New Britain. The legislation urged that cases be assigned "to a small number of judges so that a consistent body of expertise can be developed." In practice the first two dozen appeals were heard by the same two judges—with findings in over half the cases supporting the affordable housing proposal.

Connecticut's law is not going to produce affordable housing along every village lane. First, the income ceiling for buying or renting affordable housing is set at 80 percent of an area's median income (or about $29,000 for a four-person family statewide in 1990). Mortgage payments or monthly rentals cannot exceed 30 percent of family income. Second, a developer's project proposal can qualify with as few as 20 percent of the units being priced as affordable housing. Finally, communities where "assisted housing" already exceeds 10 percent of the housing supply are exempted. (Only about 25 of Connecticut's 169 towns meet or exceed this standard.) Also exempted are communities that are actively participating in Connecticut's Housing Partnership Program or Regional Fair Housing Compact Pilot Program (in the Hartford and Bridgeport areas).

Nevertheless, the Affordable Housing Land Use Appeals Procedure is a major tool for social change in Connecticut. As a Connecticut attorney notes,

> An unspoken reason for recommending the affordable housing appeals law was to encourage racial integration in Connecticut suburbs. The unequal distribution of wealth and resources caused in part by towns' exclusionary land use decisions . . . has created an imbalance between the housing needs of low-income, urban minorities and the housing opportunities of their more affluent, white, suburban neighbors. Opening up the suburbs to the full range of economic classes will, at the same time, promote racial dispersal.

2) The Winds of Regionalism   Five years after passage of the Affordable Housing Appeals Act, the state of Connecticut is moving fitfully toward another major step in forging a policy of shared responsibility among its 169 towns—regional government.

The 1990s had ushered in hard times for the state's economy. The bloom was off New England's economic miracle. The nation's second largest concentration of defense contractors, Connecticut's manufacturers had been hard hit by procurement cutbacks as the Cold War ended. In five years, the state lost 250,000 jobs from cutbacks in its bellwether insurance industry and manufacturing industries. The Census Bureau reported that from 1990 to 1993, Connecticut was the only state to lose population and that the Hartford metro area had had the highest percentage population loss.

In the state courts, a controversial lawsuit was driving political change. Parents of black and Hispanic students in Hartford had brought a suit, *Sheff* v. *O'Neill*, which challenged, in effect, Connecticut's entire system of local governance. In the face of such gaping economic and social disparities between Hartford and its suburbs, the plaintiffs claimed that organizing public education along town lines denied their children the right to education guaranteed by the state constitution. The plaintiffs claimed that Connecticut's system of town governance represented a denial of equal protection under the law for Hartford's minority school children.

There Was So Much Resistance to the Baltimore Beltway People Threatened to Lie Down in Front of the Bulldozers. Protesters Argued, "It Will Ruin the Good Life of the County."

At 3:30 p.m. on an afternoon in July of 1962, then Governor Millard Tawes—in company of reporters, TV cameras and VIP's—stood in the Beltway at the foot of the Reisterstown Road East exit. In a short dedicatory speech following a ribbon cutting, the Governor officially opened the Beltway, calling it "the greatest peacetime public works project in history," and "a giant step toward linking Baltimore's great communities"—Towson with Catonsville, Dundalk with Pikesville, Arbutus with Pikesville, and so on around. By 6 p.m. of that same day it was estimated that at least 45,000 cars a day (today the comparable figure is 156,950) would be using the thoroughfare, and there was already talk of adding a third and even fourth lane.

That is the way the Baltimore Beltway project ended, but it is not at all the way it began.

When, in 1952 or so, word had gotten out that there would be this ribbon of concrete running through all those green and lovely suburban neighborhoods, all hell broke loose. Neighbor-

hood improvement associations, one right after the other, called the plan a threat to the good life of suburbia and 10 associations banded together to form the "Civic Council." In hearing after hearing, spokespersons for the neighborhood associations argued to preserve their "good life," and vigorously denounced the plan. They shouted that they'd lie in front of the bulldozers before they would let a beltway be built.

But inexorably, the beltway was built; the first section ran from Loch Raven to the Jones Falls, then another from Route 40 to Ritchie Highway. Finally, by 1962, the entire circle, as far as it was planned to go, was completed.

Exactly one year after Governor Tawes opened the Beltway, the State Roads Commission took a door-to-door survey among the very neighborhood people who had so vociferously opposed the project in the first place. Asked if they like the Beltway, 80 percent said they loved it.

Equal protection under the law was the theme of another constitutional challenge announced by New Haven's new mayor, John DeStefano. He campaigned successfully for mayor on a platform of suing the state over the state's town-based property tax system. Once again, the theme was that such great economic disparities exist between impoverished New Haven and its suburbs that New Haven residents are denied equal protection. New Haven's high property tax rates (the state's highest) had prompted a secession movement by residents of New Haven's East Shore area. "Secede to Survive" signs dotted lawns in its middle class neighborhoods.

In such an atmosphere of civic disquiet, legislative leadership stepped forward. The co-chairs of the General Assembly's Planning and Development Committee, State Representative Jefferson Davis (D-Pomfret) and State Senator Thirman Milner (D-Hartford) organized 25 key legislators, mayors and first selectpersons, business, and labor and community leaders into a "regionalism collaborative process." In February 1994, the group called for the General Assembly to establish a system of regional governments in its 1995 session. The group's report to the legislative leadership stated:

> We have agreed there needs to be an intermediate structure between state and local government. We came to the collective belief that there are issues that transcend local boundaries. Our failure to provide ways to deal with those issues will hold back our state's potential in the 21st century. . . .
>
> Call [our proposed regional governments] an upper level of local government. Our proposal does not abolish any local government and in fact in many ways will complement and enhance it. The [regional governments'] first and foremost responsibility is policy. While greater efficiency and equity in service delivery can save money, we believe that only metro-wide policy decisions have the ability to create the dynamic that will allow the entire area to move ahead over time. Primary policy areas should be land use, housing, transportation, health, economic development and education. . . .
>
> We agreed the intermediate structures need the ability to raise revenue and recognized that funding could come from federal, state, and local levels. Funds could also be raised on a regional level and bonds could be issued. . . .
>
> We finished without time to resolve some issues such as what size the regions should be. We liked the history of counties but also recognized the strength of . . . arguments for looking at entire metropolitan areas. We agreed we wanted to work toward an elected body, but felt that [member city and town] chief elected officials might work in a transitional period.

The groups agenda has been temporarily side tracked by Republican control of the state senate. However, for a state that treasures its tradition of local "home rule" or town government perhaps beyond all other states, Connecticut's achieving such a broad consensus in favor of regionalism is, in itself, a major step forward.

B. Montgomery County, Maryland

Maryland's Montgomery County has one of the nation's most comprehensive and balanced local housing programs. Though Montgomery County is not technically a metro area itself, its housing programs operate on a scale and with a sophistication that should be applied on a metropolitan scale. The fact that such a program would exist in Montgomery County is no happenstance. Montgomery County itself is an excellent example of the social integration that can be achieved by a broad-based, unified local government with both authority and political will to pursue such policies.

A wealthy suburban county outside Washington, D.C., Montgomery County grew from 164,401 residents in 1950 to 757,027 in 1990, surpassing the nation's capital itself in total population. Standing alone, Montgomery County would be the country's 54th largest metropolitan area. The area was a prime candidate for typical suburban "balkanization."

It didn't happen. First, under Maryland state law, the county maintains a single, unified, countywide school system. With 117,086 students in 1992–1993, the Montgomery County Public Schools is one of the nation's 20th largest school system—and with a well-deserved reputation for excellence.

Second, in 1927 (later amended in 1939), the Maryland legislature established the Maryland–National Capital Park and Planning Commission and gave the Montgomery County government exclusive planning and zoning control throughout the county, except for grandfathering existing zoning powers for the cities of Rockville and Gaithersburg and five small villages (which together currently house about 12 percent of the county's population).

This legislative action created "a big enough canvas to work on," in the words of Richard Tustian, long-time county planner. The county government's wide scope of authority has led to perhaps the nation's most comprehensive growth management system. Key elements are the long-range "wedges and corridors" Comprehensive Plan; the Annual Growth Policy; the Adequate Public Facilities Ordinance (linking subdivision approval to the orderly construction of public facilities); and the Transferable Development Rights program (to preserve one-third of the county as agricultural land).

Third, beyond its planning and zoning policies, Montgomery County actively entered the housing field in 1966 when the County Council established the Housing Authority of Montgomery County (HAMC). Initially, HAMC was a traditional, federally supported public housing authority. However, coming into the field relatively late, the county housing authority was able to avoid the mistakes of earlier public housing programs, particularly a reliance on building large, higher-density projects. HAMC built conventional, but relatively small, public housing projects. These early projects ranged in size from 19–76 family units and 96–160 elderly units with two mixed family/elderly projects.

In 1974, the County Council reorganized HAMC as the Housing Opportunities Commission (HOC) and assigned the restructured agency an additional major role as the county's housing finance agency. This reorganization coincided with the creation of Montgomery County's widely acclaimed Moderately-Priced Dwelling Unit (MPDU) policy.

1) The Moderately-Priced Dwelling Unit (MPDU) Policy

At the time of its enactment in 1973, the Moderately-Priced Dwelling Unit (MPDU) Policy was believed to be the nation's only mandatory *inclusionary* zoning ordinance. The MPDU policy applies to all new, private, residential developments of 50 or more units, whether they are in single-family home subdivisions, townhouse developments, or apartment complexes. The policy mandates the creation of mixed income communities through the following formula:

a. 85 percent of all units will be "market rate"—that is, sold or rented to whatever income group the developer is targeting;

b. 10 percent must be "affordable"—that is, at purchase prices or rental levels that represent no more than 30 percent of the income of households earning no more than 80 percent of the county's median household income; and

c. *most significantly, 5 percent must be made available for direct purchase or rental by the county's Housing Opportunities Commission for placement of deep-subsidy households.*

Whenever possible, the MPDU units are indistinguishable architecturally from the market rate units. However, in a housing market as expensive as Montgomery County, some design compromises have been made for some MPDU units (though their quality remains high). To compensate developers for selling or renting 15 percent of their development at below market price, the county negotiates a density increase or "MPDU bonus" of up to 22 percent above the maximum density otherwise allowed for that zoning classification.

By 1994, a total of 9,046 housing units had been created under the MPDU policy; these included 6,376 sale units and 2,670 rental units. Faced with limitations on funds available for direct acquisition by the agency, the HOC had been able to purchase about 1,100 units (about 40 percent of their statutory allocation). To help overcome the HOC's funding shortfall, a 1989 amendment to the MPDU ordinance allowed nonprofit organizations, certified by HOC, to purchase an additional 6 2/3 percent of the MPDU units in any project for rent to additional low-income households.

The MPDU policy has provided HOC with the largest source of scattered site units for placement of deep subsidy (i.e., public-housing eligible) households. In fact, by 1994, the HOC owned so many highly scattered single-family homes, townhouses, and condominium units that, according to agency officials, HOC is paying annual membership dues to over 150 homeowner associations!

Before focusing in greater detail on HOC's programs for low-income households, it is worthwhile to examine the moderate-income clientele of the MPDU program. MPDUs must be sold to individual purchasers, not to housing speculators. Both buyers and renters are subject to maximum income limits set by the county Department of Housing and Community Development. Rent limits are controlled for 20 years. Sale and resale prices for MPDUs are controlled for ten years, and a portion of resale profits is recaptured by the County's revolving Housing Initiative Fund.

Over five recent years (1988–1992), developers working under the MPDU policy brought into being 367 rental units and 1,183 sale units. Of the new homes for sale, 14 percent had one bedroom, 24 percent had two bedrooms, and 61 percent had three bedrooms. The average sale price was $69,979—a bargain in a county where the median housing value was $208,000 in 1990.

Turning to the characteristics of MPDU home purchasers, 43 percent were white, 19 percent were black, 30 percent were Asian, and 8 percent were Hispanic. Average household income was $26,497; only 4 percent of the purchasers even approached the program's income ceiling of $39,900 for a family of four. As the county's housing finance agency, HOC facilitated many home purchases by modest-income households with special, low-interest loans and other mortgage assistance.

2) Deep-Subsidy Public Housing Programs   Turning from the county's successful moderate-income programs to its low-income program, the Housing Opportunities Commission administers the widest array of activities. HOC manages more than 1,500 rental units—555 apartments for the elderly in four complexes, 328 family or mixed family/elderly apartments in seven complexes, and 887 rental units that it owns, scattered throughout the county—and purchased through its MPDU allocation.

Some public housing residents are offered the opportunity to become homeowners of the units they rent. Two such homeownership communities are Tobytown, where, as of 1992, four of 26 units had been sold to occupants, and Bel Pre, where 36 of 50 families had become homeowners. Another 102 scattered site public housing units have been designated for occupant ownership. In 1992, all but 31 had been sold to occupants. Of 178 available units, occupants were purchasing 115, generally with assistance from the county's Homeownership Assistance Loan Fund (HALF), offering mortgages with interest as low as 6 percent.

HOC administers the county's federally funded Section 8 rental subsidy program, which partially subsidizes rents for over 3,100 families in privately owned rental housing. Once a Section 8 certificate or voucher is awarded to an eligible family, recipients locate their own homes to rent in the private marketplace. Once such a unit is found, the landlord and renter enter into a regular lease agreement. The tenants pay up to 30 percent of their income for rent; HOC pays the rest from Section 8 funds. The amount of subsidy is based on tenant incomes and expenses in accordance with federal guidelines.

HOC administers many other low-income housing assistance programs. Among them are four not-for-profit-owned apartment complexes built under the old federal Section 236 program, a variety of special programs under other aspects of the federal Section 8 program, and five joint projects with private investors utilizing the 1986 federal Low-Income Housing Tax Credit Program.

What is most important about the totality of HOC's programs is the degree to which low-income housing is spread around the county. Table 2.5 illustrates the relatively even dispersion of HOC's programs across all 18 planning districts into which the county is divided.

It is clear that the MPDU policy and scope of HOC's programs have helped the county accommodate—even encourage—a remarkable social transformation. In 1970, Montgomery County had the look of a classic suburb—wealthy and white (92 percent). By 1990, Montgomery County had a "rainbow" look—73 percent white, 12

TABLE 2.5
Distribution of assisted housing units in Montgomery County

Planning District	HOC-Assisted Rental Units	% of All HOC-Assisted Rental Units	HOC Units as % of All Rental Units	HOC Units as % of All Units
Aspen Hill	1,507	14.9%	22.3%	6.8%
Bethesda CBD	203	2.0%	5.2%	4.2%
Bethesda/Chevy Chase	12	0.1%	0.2%	0.0%
Cloverly	148	1.5%	32.0%	3.1%
Damascus	140	1.4%	26.8%	4.1%
Fairland/White Oaks	954	9.4%	9.8%	3.8%
Gaithersburg East	1,384	13.6%	11.4%	4.4%
Gaithersburg West	547	5.4%	11.2%	3.5%
Germantown East	279	2.7%	19.2%	6.1%
Germantown West	386	3.8%	8.2%	2.8%
Kensington/Wheaton	1,009	9.9%	10.3%	2.8%
North Bethesda	357	3.5%	5.9%	2.2%
Olney	157	1.5%	18.0%	1.9%
Potomac	460	4.5%	27.2%	3.0%
Rockville	832	8.2%	13.7%	4.9%
Rural	151	1.5%	9.9%	1.2%
Silver Spring CBD	501	4.9%	11.7%	11.6%
Silver Spring/Tacoma Park	1,087	10.7%	7.0%	3.9%
County totals	**10,114**	**100.0%**	**10.5%**	**3.4%**

percent black, 7 percent Hispanic, and 8 percent Asian, a better reflection of the region's racial percentages. While maintaining its preeminence as one of the country's ten richest urban counties, Montgomery County also has a rich diversity of income groups.

Montgomery County's housing programs and policies can serve as a state-of-the-art model for metro Baltimore.

2. Metropolitan Revenue Sharing

A. Twin Cities Fiscal Disparities Plan

The most significant example of metropolitan tax sharing in the United States, or, more accurately, tax *base* sharing, is the Twin Cities Fiscal Disparities Plan in the Minneapolis–St. Paul area enacted by the Minnesota legislature in 1971.

The Twin Cities Metropolitan Council has described the plan's rationale very succinctly:

> From a regional perspective the Twin Cities is one economy. Large commercial-industrial developments tend to concentrate in a few loca-

tions, drawing workers and clients from a market area that is larger than the city it is located in. Access to these concentrations, primarily highways, is a prime determinant of where these developments locate. Cities with such access are the ones most likely to get commercial-industrial development.

Since the property tax is the primary source of local government revenues, certain types of development—office space, headquarters buildings, upscale housing—are attractive because they typically generate more revenue than it costs to serve them. Not all cities can expect to attract such development, but most participate in financing the regional facilities serving these developments. The idea underlying tax-base sharing is to allow all cities to share in the commercial-industrial development that is, to a large extent, the result of the regional market and public investments made at the regional and state levels.

Under the state law, the plan applies to 187 municipalities in the seven-county Twin Cities area. Since 1971, 40 percent of the *increase* in the assessed value of commercial-industrial property has been allocated into a common pool. (A city's pre-1971 assessed valuation is exempted.) The revenues from the pool are then redistributed among all 187 municipalities on the basis of annual estimated population figures and how each city's per capita property value compares with the metro-wide per capita value.

By 1995, the annual "fiscal disparities" fund amounted to $241 million, almost 27 percent of the region's $906 million in commercial-industrial property tax collections. Some 140 communities were net recipients, while 47 were net contributors.

Over the years, the net contributors have consistently been the Twin Cities' wealthiest suburbs, such as Bloomington, Minnetonka, Eden Prairie, Plymouth, and Edina. Giant shopping malls, office towers, and gardenlike industrial parks have sprouted vigorously along the interstate highways that cut through these suburbs or adjacent to the suburban Minneapolis–St. Paul International Airport.

Major recipients have been the City of St. Paul; many older, inner suburbs in Hennepin and Ramsey Counties; and virtually all towns and villages lying well beyond the suburban beltways.

Fueled by its downtown office boom, Minneapolis went from being the largest net recipient in 1980 to the region's largest net contributor. Its $19 million net contribution in 1991 represented 6.5 percent of its commercial-industrial tax capacity. With the recent decline in the downtown office market, however, Minneapolis has moved back into becoming a net recipient from the fund.

The tax base sharing program is successfully reducing fiscal disparities. A Citizens League Study has found that, among 56 communities with 3,000 or more households, the ratio of richest to poorest community would be 17 to 1, as measured by per capita commercial-industrial property value. The Fiscal Disparities Plan has reduced the ratio to 4 to 1.

By 1993, however, though the Fiscal Disparities Plan itself had worked well, discontent was growing with the overall performance of the Metropolitan Council. Throughout the 1970s, the Metropolitan Council had been very aggressive in promoting moderate-income housing in suburban areas. Its principal tool had been use of federal housing funds, primarily the Section 236 program. However, when the Reagan Administration cut back on federal housing programs, the Metropolitan Council did not seek to fill the incentive gap through new state or locally based policies and programs. In fact, the Metropolitan Council lost momentum on all fronts as a succession of more conservative governors filled the council with appointees who lacked earlier appointees' zeal for forging metropolitan cooperation.

Throughout the 1980s, therefore, the Twin Cities area followed the same path as many inelastic metro areas, becoming a metropolitan society organized increasingly by income class—with most of the growth occurring in the so-called "Fertile Crescent" (wealthier suburbs to the south and west of Minneapolis–St. Paul).

Twin Cities' leaders were shocked to realize that, as is evident in the 1990 census, both cities were going steadily down the path of inner-city decline from which many thought the Twin Cities were exempt. In just ten years, for example, minority student enrollment in the Minneapolis Public Schools rose from 20 percent to 50 percent, and the number of students qualifying for free school lunches rose from 30 percent to 60 percent.

But with its strong civic culture, the Twin Cities area was quick to respond. State Representative Myron Orfield (Minneapolis) forged a powerful legislative coalition among city legislators, legislators from older, inner-ring suburbs that are now experiencing the rapid increase in "inner-city" problems, and rural Farmer-Labor Democrats. In 1993 they successfully passed a wide-ranging package of metropolitan reform bills under the umbrella of the Metropolitan Communities Stabilization Act. Unfortunately, the coalition lacked one crucial vote: Independent-Republican Governor Arne Carlson, who voted against most of the package at the behest of Fertile Crescent constituents.

In the veto's aftermath, both sides came together to form the Advisory Council on Metropolitan Governance (co-chaired by Orfield). In March 1994, it issued its report, calling for direct election of the Metropolitan Council and significantly strengthening its powers. Three major regional agencies—transit, transportation planning, and regional sewage treatment—would be folded under the Metropolitan Council as operating divisions, and a fourth would be created to handle metropolitan housing and redevelopment programs.

Simultaneously, the legislative coalition renewed its proposals for fair share affordable housing requirements for all suburban communities. They also introduced proposals to expand the Fiscal Disparities Plan to include residential housing. Forty percent of the tax base from all residential properties over $150,000 in value (about 50 percent above the regional median) would be pooled along with commercial and industrial property. The action would create a $100 million annual fund for the Metropolitan Council's new housing and redevelopment division. One-third would be allocated to communities that had not yet met their affordable housing requirements; two-thirds would be directed toward redevelopment of depressed inner-city and older suburban neighborhoods.

Balance and stability, State Representative Orfield states, are the key themes in forging a community of interest between central cities and older suburbs.

CONCLUSIONS: WHAT LESSONS DO THE MODELS TEACH?

In this chapter, I have sketched a varied mix of strategies that have allowed central cities to cope successfully with the constant outward expansion of urban development. Some strategies (such as annexation or formal city-county consolidation) allow the city itself to capture its share of growth by expanding the city's boundaries. Other strategies help central cities minimize their potential social and fiscal isolation within growing suburban communities. Such models include two-tier governments (empowered urban counties, metropolitan councils) or state government–imposed responsibilities to share central city burdens (fair share affordable housing, tax base sharing). Before we look specifically at what models might be most applicable to metro Baltimore, what general lessons can be derived from these case studies?

Lesson 1: State Government Must Play the Key Role

As was noted in the discussion of Metro Toronto, under the Canadian constitution, provincial governments have full authority over the conduct of local government affairs. Under the U.S. Constitution, state governments have the same authority. The U.S. Constitution is silent on the issue of local government; therefore, under the Tenth Amendment, determining the form and power of local government is a power reserved to the states.

The problem is that U.S. legislatures rarely exercise that authority to deal with the growing complexity of governance in metropolitan areas. Typically, legislatures give considerable deference to local governments and local authority, heavily influenced by the American enshrinement of "home rule." By contrast, Canadian provincial governments are much more robust in the exercise of their constitutional responsibilities. Provincial governments not only established Metro Toronto (further combining and reorganizing local governments in the process), but also decreed regional arrangements for Montreal, Winnipeg, Edmonton, Vancouver, and several other Canadian urban areas.

Nevertheless, in the United States, despite the reluctance of state legislators, regional progress has occurred when legislators have either made it happen or set up favorable ground rules to encourage local reform. In particular, regional progress occurs when

- *State laws favor municipal annexation.* The North Carolina legislature, for instance, gave its major cities the power of "involuntary" annexation (that is, the power to annex over the objections of property owners and county government if necessary). Furthermore, the legislature gave North Carolina's cities the ability to minimize suburban fragmentation through their veto power over incorporation of nearby areas into new municipalities. The legislature virtually guaranteed that North Carolina will have strong, healthy cities serving as powerful engines of regional economic growth.

- *Legislatively established ground rules facilitate consolidation.* Nashville–Davidson County and Jacksonville–Duval County were consolidated by popular vote because state laws prevented voters in smaller jurisdictions from exercising a veto over the countywide majority. The Indiana legislature consolidated Indianapolis–Marion County by direct legislative act—the only such consolidation without a popular vote in this century.

- *Metropolitan governments are established by direct legislative act,* such as Portland's Metro and the Twin Cities' Metropolitan Council. Legislatures have used such bodies as instruments to carry out state laws such as Oregon's Growth Management Act and Minnesota's Fiscal Disparities Plan.
- *State law requires local governments to share responsibility for critical social problems.* The State of Connecticut's Affordable Housing Appeals Process is an excellent example.

For three decades, troubled cities have looked to the federal government for help. Their gaze is misdirected. The nation's metropolitan regions are wealthier than the nation's debt-burdened federal government. Many of American cities' problems are structural. State legislatures hold the keys to reorganizing urban governance effectively.

Lesson 2: Metropolitan Institutions Must Be Flexible Geographically to Adapt to Long-term Growth Trends

If anything, this lesson is derived from the shortcomings of each of the examples cited of metropolitan governance:

- Despite its well-deserved fame, Metro Toronto's jurisdictional area now covers only about half the population and one-tenth of the land area of the Greater Toronto Region. In effect, the City of Toronto is a medium-sized U.S. city. The 240-square-mile Metro Toronto is still smaller geographically than Anchorage, Dallas, Fort Worth, Houston, Indianapolis, Jacksonville, Lexington, Los Angeles, Memphis, Nashville, New York City, Virginia Beach, Oklahoma City, Phoenix, San Antonio, and San Diego—all of which have greater "unitary" powers over their jurisdictions than Metro Toronto does. The regional municipalities in the Greater Toronto Area are, in effect, medium-sized U.S. suburban counties.
- Portland Metro must contend with the fact that a significant portion of its metro area (i.e., Clark County, Washington) is in another state. Quasi-metropolitan King County covers only 75 percent of the population of its metro area (and only 60 percent of the consolidated area with Tacoma–Pierce County). By 1990, growth in the Twin Cities region had expanded beyond the Metropolitan Council's seven-county jurisdiction to include another four counties.

- Upon their successful city-county consolidations, Jacksonville, Indianapolis, and Nashville all totally dominated their defined metro areas. By the 1990 census, each was a slowly declining share of its growing metro area: Jacksonville, 70 percent of four counties; Indianapolis, 60 percent of eight counties; and Nashville, 50 percent of eight counties. To perpetuate past successes, each consolidated city-county must strengthen cooperative efforts with neighboring counties or send their state legislatures back to the drawing board.

In short, the geography of metropolitan governance cannot be cast in stone—or, better said, in metes and bounds. The low-density patterns of urban growth will render fixed, unadjustable boundaries for metropolitan governance increasingly obsolete.

Lesson 3: Growth Management Policies Are Important Tools to Promote Social Equity

Inner-city black ghettos and Hispanic barrios are also the by-products of ever-outward patterns of urban sprawl. In essence, suburban sprawl encourages abandonment of inner-city neighborhoods. Growth management policies are needed to help promote social equity.

Dr. Thomas Bier at Cleveland State University's Urban Center has analyzed the relationship between the supply of new housing (net housing starts) and the demands for new housing (net household formation) in Ohio's metro areas to understand the fiscal and environmental costs of sprawl. Most new housing starts are in upper-end subdivisions that are increasingly farther out on the metropolitan periphery; few new housing units are built within central cities. However, in many metro areas, the building industry is creating more housing than is required by net household formation. The newest, high-end housing always sells, prompting successive waves of homeowners to "move up" (in price) but also "move out" (of inner cities and older, blue collar suburbs.) The net surplus of housing over demand causes the economic abandonment of otherwise sound housing in the urban core. The net effect is the systematic depopulation of central cities.

Table 2.6 summarizes the results of the supply of and demand for new housing in Ohio's metropolitan areas. The second and third columns relate the degree of imbalance in new housing supply/net household formation to net city population change. The fourth and fifth columns relate these changes to trends in the ratio of city per capita incomes to suburban per capita incomes.

TABLE 2.6
Metro-wide housing supply/demand imbalances in Ohio

City	Ratio of New Units to Household Growth, 1980s	Change in Central City Households, 1980s	Change in City/Suburb Income Ratio, 1980s	City/ Suburb Income Ratio, 1989
Columbus	1.0	23.6%	−3.6%	81.3%
Cincinnati	1.2	−0.5%	−6.7%	82.0%
Dayton	1.6	−7.4%	−10.0%	64.1%
Akron	1.7	−1.5%	−6.9%	76.1%
Cleveland	1.8	−5.8%	−9.6%	53.5%
Youngstown	2.3	−7.3%	−18.9%	63.9%
Toledo	2.5	−1.3%	−12.3%	72.2%

Dr. Bier notes that in four of the cities, population decline was reduced or avoided:

- In Columbus [Ohio's only high elasticity city], 59.1 percent of all housing units built in the metropolitan area were located in the city, enabling the city to grow in population. (Columbus' new construction was located mainly in former suburbs that had been annexed by the city.)
- Construction in the city of Cincinnati was a small portion (5.6 percent) of the metropolitan area, but the total amount in the area was nearly in balance with household growth (which was not the case in the other areas, except Columbus).
- Akron [a low elasticity city] reduced its population loss through annexation.
- The city of Toledo has 22.9 percent of all new housing in its area, thus reducing its population decline. If construction in Toledo had been at the rate of Cleveland, Youngstown, or Dayton (3–4 percent), the city's population loss would have been 50 percent greater.

The most effective programs to promote broader geographic re-settlement of poor minorities are complemented by growth management programs. Such programs contribute to maintaining the value and desirability of older, central city neighborhoods for middle class households by controlling and targeting new housing development.

Of the cities studied, Toronto is the best example of policies combining scattered public housing with policies to strengthen middle class city neighborhoods. Though not a central city, with its highly varied population of 757,000, Montgomery County has shown how a comprehensive program of growth management, combined with enlightened housing policies, can maintain housing values in all areas of the county and prevent any one neighborhood from becoming a slum.

Lesson 4: Direct Election of Metropolitan Officials Is Desirable

In part, this is another lesson that is drawn primarily from negative experiences. As regional bodies, voluntary councils of governments rarely tackle tough social issues. Their ruling bodies are composed of elected officials of member counties and municipalities. However strong their commitment to regional cooperation, their primary allegiance is to the voters of the jurisdiction who elected them to the public office that is the basis of their membership in the council of governments. This allegiance militates against many elected officials tackling the hard-core issues of race and class that a presumed majority of their constituents don't want addressed in any way that involves apparent sacrifice on their part.

There has been a gradual trend away from federative (or appointive) bodies to metropolitan structures whose governing bodies are directly elected. The Oregon legislature provided direct elections for Portland Metro in 1977. Metro citizens confirmed that arrangement in adopting a home rule charter in 1992. King County voters merged the Seattle Metro into King County government, replacing an unwieldy federated board with the directly elected Metropolitan County Council of King County. In 1988, the Ontario parliament set aside a 35-year tradition of a federative Metropolitan Council in favor of direct election within 32 wards apportioned throughout Metro Toronto. In 1994, the Minnesota legislature failed by one vote to change its gubernatorially appointed Metropolitan Council into a directly elected body.

In each instance, the changeover has been motivated by the need to comply with "one person, one vote" constitutional requirements and the desire to strengthen political accountability. Yet the public record is replete with instances in which direct referendum has resulted in the defeat of many of the strategies discussed above. (For example, city-county consolidation proposals have been rejected over 100 times since World War II—five defeats for each success.) Why should any confidence be placed in direct election of metro officials to carry out policies that might well be rejected by the general population if submitted to referendum?

First, those who present themselves as candidates for public office generally believe in the mission of that office. Candidates typically are not motivated to undermine the office to which they are elected to serve (recent conservative rhetoric notwithstanding). If the mission of a Metropolitan Council—however controversial—is established by state law, for instance, those who run and serve generally seek to advance the organization's mission. Support for the mission has been the experience to date, for example, with directly elected officials of Portland Metro and Metro Toronto.

Second, a vital factor in securing broad public support for controversial programs and policies is the public perception (which must be based on reality) that the programs or policies are being applied fairly and evenhandedly. Fairness and uniformity have allowed the Montgomery County Council to stand behind its Moderately-Priced Dwelling Unit Plan. That concern—maintaining evenhanded application of the policy—caused the Council in 1992 to demand construction of MPDUs (including the normal set-aside for public housing households) in the Avenel subdivision, one of Montgomery County's wealthiest areas.

Third, systems of representation on metropolitan bodies can be devised that represent a cross section of all segments of the metro community rather than creating districts with sharply different interests. Indeed, it is the broad-based, more comprehensive nature of elastic cities and fully empowered counties that allows them generally to move beyond highly parochial concerns and embrace communitywide policies and programs.

Thus, as we seek to devise a strategy for metro Baltimore in the next chapter, we can adopt these guideposts: state legislative role, geographic flexibility, a comprehensive approach that combines growth management and social equity policies, and direct election of metro officials.

CHAPTER THREE

THE STRATEGY

Chapter One analyzed the necessity of reversing Baltimore City's growing social and economic isolation as an inelastic central city is cut off from its region's growth. Chapter Two outlined various alternative techniques that different communities have used to maintain a city's social and economic balance. Beyond formally changing a city's jurisdictional boundaries, these techniques included functional policies (housing policies, tax-sharing policies, etc.) that help to prevent the central city's isolation. This chapter will assess the applicability of the various techniques to the Baltimore area and then recommend a specific strategy for Baltimore City and its surrounding jurisdictions.

THE ESSENTIAL GOAL: MORE EVEN DISTRIBUTION OF POOR MINORITIES

The central issue hampering the Baltimore region is severe racial and economic segregation that is isolating the City of Baltimore and that will ultimately drag the entire region down with it. To Baltimore City is consigned the role of being the metro area's poorhouse.

For the city, the fiscal consequences are obvious. The poor need the most public services but pay the least taxes. City government struggles constantly with the gap between needs and resources. In addition, the concentration of poverty in isolated neighborhoods makes social and economic progress difficult.

Many see central city problems largely in terms of *fiscal* disparities and pursue *fiscal* remedies. Big city mayors are constantly seeking more federal aid. In FY 1991, almost 18 percent of Baltimore City's revenues came from federal grants-in-aid, yet since the end of general revenue sharing in 1984, few federal dollars directly support what would traditionally be viewed as basic city services. Though vital to community welfare, many federally supported social welfare programs would disappear if federal funds supporting them dried up.

Maryland state government itself serves as a further vehicle to cushion Baltimore City's built-in fiscal crisis. In FY 1991, direct state aid was 29 percent of the city's budget. Without state aid, Baltimore City would be bankrupt.

Maryland state government also subsidizes Baltimore City residents indirectly. Since 1851, Baltimore City has been an "independent city"—that is, the city is not part of a larger county, but its city government carries out all the functions and responsibilities of county government. Thus, not being part of a larger county, Baltimore City does not have a larger tax base to draw on to support county functions (particularly in social services, public health, and criminal justice). However, state subsidy of health and welfare services as well as the services provided directly by state agencies are a form of fiscal subsidy for Baltimore City.

Elastic cities are fiscally stronger. Through annexation or city-county consolidation, elastic cities have incorporated a large share of their region's growth within their expanded city limits. Other fiscal strategies (most notably the Twin Cities Fiscal Disparities Plan) are targeted on easing the fiscal crunch on inelastic communities.

However, when a city and its neighborhoods, like Baltimore City, become highly impacted by high concentrations of poor households, there is no feasible amount of money that can make a significant difference. The very concentration of poverty itself becomes the enemy, making social programs less effective in alleviating the effects of poverty. It takes exponentially more money to address the effects of poverty in neighborhoods where poverty is highly concentrated because social problems are compounded. Reducing fiscal disparities between Baltimore City and its suburbs would be a valuable side effect of strategies to regain Baltimore City's social balance. A purely fiscal strategy, however, cannot be the main line of attack on Baltimore City's problems.

The central goal must be to end Baltimore City's role as the metro area's poorhouse. Action must be taken to diminish significantly the intense concentration of poor people (particularly, as will be shown, of poor black people) in certain Baltimore City neighborhoods. Large numbers of poor households must be offered the opportunity to relocate from poverty-impacted neighborhoods to predominantly middle class neighborhoods.

The term "relocation" in this discussion means both the creation of choice (through MPDU-type housing development policies) and the exercise of choice voluntarily (by the heads of poor households). The lesson of experience is that, given the opportunity, a majority of poor black household heads will choose to move to better neighborhoods, including to predominantly white subur-

THE BEGINNINGS OF "BWI INTERNATIONAL" Go Back More Than Half a Century— to "Friendship" and Baltimore Municipal Airport Before That. The Planners Bet That Air Travel Would Take Off!

Today, out of what is known as Baltimore-Washington International Airport, there are planes taking off for 80 destinations across America and around the world. The "BWI" terminal occupies almost a million square feet on 3,200 acres; its parking lots accommodate 10,000 cars: it manages 600 arrivals and departures a day—through 47 jet gates and 18 commuter gates.

The whole complex of counters, ramps, runways, luggage terminals, and restaurants (12 of them) is bewildering, massive, overwhelming. Time, then, to recall Baltimore Municipal Airport.

From 1941 to 1950 (when Friendship, later BWI, opened), Baltimore Municipal Airport occupied the acreage in Dundalk that then and now abuts Broening Highway (about where Colgate Creek meets the Patapsco River).

The site today is the Dundalk Marine Terminal. Municipal took over as Baltimore's airport from little old Logan Field, which was across the road to the west and is now the Logan Shopping Center. (When Friendship opened, the city fathers renamed Municipal the Harbor Field.)

But in its glory days, from 1941 until the 1950s, Municipal was Baltimore's airport. It was used by the modest number of Baltimoreans who in those pre-jet days chose to fly instead of taking the train.

The airport and the airlines serving it, including American, Eastern, United, Pan Am, and British Overseas Airways (to Bermuda) shared a wild dream: They were betting that airline (including seaplane) travel would help shape the world of tomorrow.

Guests who visited the airport's terminal building in its opening days were rhapsodic about it. One noted:

It's smaller than but more tastefully designed and decorated than New York City's LaGuardia. Sunlight streams into the rotunda from dozen high narrow windows. The floor is covered with quarry tile in a pastel red: the baseboard is deep blue, the walls are beige tile. The woodwork is a pale blue pastel.

In 1936 Pan Am designated Municipal as the hub of its trans-Atlantic seaplane operations. Glenn Martin, whose company
Continued on page 82

ban areas. For example, the nation's oldest, largest housing choice program for poor households is the Chicago-based Gautreaux Project. Under federal court order, over 5,000 public housing tenants have been enabled to move out of South Chicago's notorious high-rise projects into rent-subsidized private housing. Almost all are black, single mother–headed families. The vouchers can be used for private rentals either within the city of Chicago or anywhere in Chicago's six surrounding counties.

Over two-thirds of the families relocated to suburban areas, experiencing substantially better educational and employment income than did families that remained in city neighborhoods. The program makes 500 new rent vouchers a year available. The program has become so popular that annual enrollment is now conducted by a "phone lottery." Applicants must call a special phone number on one day a year. Those whose calls are routed electronically through the switchboard are automatically enrolled. The telephone company estimates the Gautreaux Project switchboard receives 15,000 attempted calls on Enrollment Day!

In elastic cities (and their metro areas), poor people are typically more evenly distributed throughout their jurisdictions—though none of the other communities that are compared with Baltimore in Chapter One nor those cited as models in Chapter Two has pursued social balance with the comprehensive approach of Montgomery County.

The challenge is how to design a canvas large enough to work on. And, having identified that canvas, what mechanisms would be desirable to carry out the necessary policies? Would the goal be met by:

- expanding Baltimore City through renewed annexation?
- redefining the City through city-county consolidation?
- devising a strategy in which the metro area would not *be* one government but in which the existing governments would have to *act* like one government in dealing with concentrated poverty?
- or shifting the problem entirely to state government?

Whatever the strategy or mechanism, a more even distribution of Baltimore City's poor throughout the metro area will lower the overall level of crime and delinquency, dependency, and family disintegration. It will also probably lower the level of poverty itself areawide. Success will also restore greater fiscal and economic health to the core city. Baltimore City can then become a more powerful engine of economic growth for the entire region—from which, once again, the entire region will benefit.

THE BEGINNINGS OF "BWI INTERNATIONAL"
(continued)

was building the famous Clipper seaplanes, said at the time: "Baltimore will face a golden opportunity of becoming a world port."

So promising was Municipal that the German Zeppelin company was thinking of flying dirigibles out of the facility. The war made seaplanes obsolete and dashed Baltimore's dream of becoming the leading seaplane port of the world.

Many Baltimoreans remember flying out of Municipal. Jerold C. ("Chuck") Hoffberger (former chairman of the National Brewery) recalls how Municipal, or at least the view from over it, helped shape Baltimore's image:

Early in the 1950s we had just taken off—Dawson Farber, Sydney Marcus and myself from the brewery, and Wilfred Doner and Herbert Fried from W.B. Doner, our advertising agency. The airport was right on the water's edge, and it was a brilliant, sunlit day. I remarked on what a gorgeous sight Baltimore was—spread out in the sunshine below. Doner picked up on that. He said, "This place looks like the land of pleasant living."

You know the rest of that story.

Albert Sehlstedt, Jr., who covered aviation for *The Baltimore Sun* flew out of Municipal often on assignment, usually to Florida.

He recalls:

It looked like a "Lindbergh" airport. By that I mean it was of 1940s' vintage, with one of those chain-link fences around it, protecting passengers from the tarmac. The terminal was a domed, art deco building. I remember it as small and sort of intimate. They maybe had 20 or so arrivals and departures a day. Thinking back on it, the pace of the place seemed so slow.

Robert Rappaport used the airport to fly to Syracuse University, where he was a student. "I flew Eastern," he said. "They gave you a box lunch for a dollar. Hard-boiled egg, a chicken sandwich and an apple. Maybe a cookie."

If you want to measure how the region has changed in 45 years, compare Municipal Airport circa 1950 (20 arrivals and departures a day) with BWI in 1995: 700.

Or better still, think about Mr. Rappaport's hard-boiled egg and chicken sandwich lunch for a dollar.

STRATEGIES THAT WON'T WORK NOW IN BALTIMORE

1. Expanding Baltimore City through Annexation—Too Little, Too Late

Almost all cities were elastic in their youth. For almost 200 years, Baltimore City expanded rapidly (see Map 3.1). Through successive annexations, Baltimore City grew from just 60 acres in 1730 to 80.8 square miles by 1990. The city's last annexation took place in 1918, when it annexed almost 50 square miles of Baltimore and Anne Arundel Counties, adding 100,000 new residents and almost tripling the city's territory.

As was noted in Chapter One, however, in 1948 Maryland voters approved a constitutional amendment (Article XIII, Sec. 1) preventing Baltimore City from any further annexation without the approval of the residents of the area to be annexed. As a practical political matter, it would be nearly impossible to convince the state's voters today to repeal that amendment. (Voters do not readily surrender the appurtenances of popular sovereignty.)

MAP 3.1
Baltimore City's annexations
1730–1918

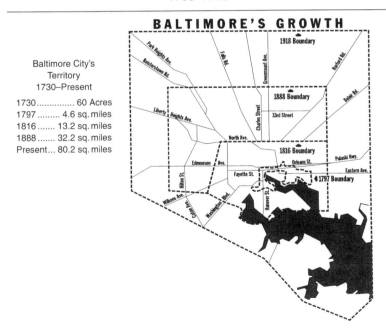

Baltimore City's
Territory
1730–Present

1730 .... 60 Acres
1797 .... 4.6 sq. miles
1816 .... 13.2 sq. miles
1888 .... 32.2 sq. miles
Present... 80.2 sq. miles

Map Courtesy of *Warfield's* Business Record

TABLE 3.1

Baltimore City's population characteristics and per capita income after
hypothetical annexation of parts of Baltimore County (1990 data)

Community	Total Population	% Black Population	% Poor Population	Per Capita Income
Baltimore City	736,104	59%	22%	$11,994
Baltimore County (inside Beltway + western Dundalk)	252,234	14%	6%	$16,236
Expanded Baltimore City total	988,338	48%	17%	$13,077

It would also be impossible to convince residents of adjacent
areas of Baltimore County and Anne Arundel County to agree to
annexation to the city. Adjacent areas are almost fully built up. They
are fully served with utilities, streets, and other urban facilities and
services by the counties.[1] The common reason why residents of developing areas voluntarily seek annexation—better facilities and
services—is moot. Annexing voluntarily into Baltimore City would
be perceived as simply marrying into a troubled family.

Moreover, even if such annexations were politically feasible,
they would not transform the economic, social, and fiscal position
of Baltimore City today. Table 3.1 suggests what Baltimore City
might gain if it successfully annexed, for example, all portions of
Baltimore County lying within the Beltway plus the western areas
of Dundalk—an annexation that would almost double the city's
area. Compared to the present Baltimore City, the areas annexed
would already have 252,000 residents, who would be predominantly white (86 percent versus 40 percent in Baltimore City),
with fewer poor residents (6 percent versus 22 percent), and with
one-third higher income levels ($16,236 versus $11,994). Such an
annexation would achieve a substantial transfusion of middle class
residents into Baltimore City.

The problem is that this demographic transfusion would not
change the essential profile of Baltimore as an old city in slow decline. Also, it simply would not break up the concentration of poor
neighborhoods. Initially, its total population would return to
slightly above 1950 levels, but within its metropolitan area, the expanded city would still be almost twice as black and twice as poor
as its metro area as a whole. The expanded city's per capita income

---

[1]There are no incorporated municipalities in Baltimore County nor, except for Annapolis City
and tiny Highland Beach (102 residents), in Anne Arundel County.

($13,077) would still be only 68 percent of readjusted suburban levels ($19,109).

In effect, with this hypothetical annexation, Baltimore City would have achieved only what the City of Richmond achieved in 1970–an annexation that would temporarily slow, but not reverse, its decline as a central city.[2]

In 1950, Baltimore City's population was 949,708, Baltimore County's was 270,273, and Anne Arundel County's was 117,392. Baltimore City's population was 71 percent of its three-county metropolitan area. Rejecting the constitutional amendment in 1948 and allowing Baltimore City to continue to annex new development would have substantially transformed its future. Four decades later, that opportunity is gone. A strategy of resuming annexation (even if politically achievable) would be too little, too late.

2. Redefining Baltimore City through City-County Consolidation—Stemming but Still Not Reversing the Decline

Consolidating Baltimore City with all of Baltimore County would be much more promising. The same constitutional amendment adopted in 1948 (Article XIII, Sec. 1) would apply to city-county consolidation. That article states that the boundary lines of a county or Baltimore City may not be changed without the consent of a majority of voters residing within the district to be annexed. Maryland law is otherwise silent on the issue of city-county consolidation, since that constitutional provision appears to preclude such action even by direct legislative statute (as occurred in the case of Indianapolis–Marion County).

An intriguing possibility has been raised by Theo Lippman, Jr., a Baltimore journalist, in *The Baltimore Sun*. Although the ar-

---

[2]In 1970, Richmond annexed 23 miles of neighboring Chesterfield County. Black plaintiffs sued to block the annexation, charging that by adding 47,000 new residents (97 percent white), the white-controlled city government was seeking to dilute growing black political power. Proponents argued that the annexation would strengthen Richmond's middle class and its tax base and would provide vacant land for future industrial, commercial, and residential growth. By unanimous vote, the U.S. Supreme Court ruled in 1975 that the annexation "was infected by the impermissible purpose of denying the right to vote based on race." The court allowed the annexation to stand, however, on the basis of Richmond's shift to a nine-member council elected by wards. Blacks gained a majority of council seats by 1978, electing Henry Marsh as Richmond's first black mayor. The irony is that both sides were correct. The 1970 annexation marked the end of Richmond's expansion. However unenthusiastic Richmond's black majority might have been regarding further annexations, in 1979 the Virginia General Assembly foreclosed the possibility by exempting urban counties from further annexations without county approval. Over the last two decades, Richmond's three adjacent counties have almost doubled in population with 221,000 new residents. However, since the 1970 demographic infusion, Richmond's population has dropped by 46,000 people (19 percent). City incomes have dropped to 83 percent of suburban incomes.

ticle was perhaps written with tongue in cheek, it is nevertheless worth analyzing. Lippman pointed out that an advisory opinion of Maryland's attorney general in 1982 held that " 'in a proposed change of county boundary lines, the controlling referendum is to be held *only* [emphasis added] in the area of a county that is to be ceded to another county.' (Constitutionally, Baltimore City is a county.)"

Lippman observed that "under the attorney general's opinion, as I read it, if Baltimore City wants to be annexed to Baltimore County—to be the annexee rather than the annexor—the General Assembly would order a referendum *only in the city*. County voters would have nothing to say about it." Lippman urged that the General Assembly authorize such a vote, if only initially a "straw vote."[3]

It is an intriguing notion—a reverse twist on a state law intended for one purpose but used for the opposite and contrary result.[4] Whether the General Assembly would authorize such a vote by Baltimore City is problematic. Many Baltimore County legislators would resist, reflecting many county residents' antipathy toward the black-dominated city and its problems. Many Baltimore City legislators might also oppose such authorization, reflecting the fears of many black city leaders (and some black residents) about the "dilution" of black voting power. Thus, enacting a "Unigov" for Baltimore City-County would probably have to be the work of the 70 percent of the General Assembly that does *not* exclusively represent either Baltimore City or Baltimore County.

The motivation of such a non-Baltimore legislative majority, however, would be that a consolidated Baltimore City–Baltimore County would be a much stronger community economically and, arguably, less dependent on state support (Table 3.2). A Baltimore Unigov would embrace an area of 680 square miles, making it the

---

[3]Lippman further observed that if a "straw vote" showed that some city neighborhoods might have the "urge to merge" and others might not, "the General Assembly could respond accordingly." Piecemeal mergers would be very injurious, since many more affluent, largely white neighborhoods in North Baltimore might prefer to join the county. More and more "secession" movements are springing up around the country (e.g., tiny Long Island, which seceded from Portland, Maine, on July 4, 1993; Staten Island and Queens seeking to secede from New York City; the East Shore district from New Haven). Secession of prosperous neighborhoods would complete Baltimore City's racial and economic isolation.

[4]Another example of a statutory reverse twist occurred in Virginia in 1964. The Virginia General Assembly had passed general authorizing legislation to facilitate the proposed consolidation of the City of Richmond with Henrico County, an action that never occurred. However, Sidney Kellam, a political boss of the Tidewater area, used the new state law to consolidate suburban Princess Anne county with the tiny city of Virginia Beach. By municipalizing the county, Kellam forestalled any further annexation of county territory by the City of Norfolk. The tactic was quickly used to create other "cities" of Chesapeake and Suffolk, in effect locking Norfolk and Portsmouth up tight within an iron ring of municipalized suburban counties.

TABLE 3.2
Baltimore's population characteristics and per capita income after a
hypothetical consolidation of Baltimore City and County (1990 data)

Community	City Area (sq. mi.)	Total Population	% Black Population	% Poor Population	Per Capita Income
Baltimore City	81	736	59%	22%	$11,994
Baltimore County	599	693	12%	6%	$18,658
Consolidated City-County	680	1,429	36%	14%	$15,226

country's third largest major municipality (after 1,698-square-mile
Anchorage and 739-square-mile Jacksonville). It would have a
combined population of 1.4 million people, making it the nation's
sixth most populous city (after New York, Los Angeles, Chicago,
Houston, and Philadelphia). As a consolidated city-county, its economic indicators would compare favorably with the Indianapolis
Unigov (14 percent poor compared with 12 percent poor for Indianapolis and $15,226 per capita compared with $14,478 for Indianapolis).[5] The ratio of consolidated city income ($15,226) to
suburban income ($18,653) would be 82 percent (compared with
a 90 percent city/suburb ratio for Indianapolis). Clearly, with good
municipal management, a Baltimore Unigov would be able to finance needed facilities and services from its expanded tax base
without having to look for increasing subsidies from state government, as Baltimore City must do now.

As shown in Table 3.3, relatively few poor blacks live in Baltimore County. Black migration into Baltimore County has been
primarily by middle class black families. Baltimore County has almost as many poor whites as Baltimore City does. However, poor
whites constitute only 5 percent of the white population in Baltimore County and are highly dispersed around the county. In only
one of the 244 census tracts in Baltimore County is there a high
concentration of poor whites—a neighborhood in Essex where 33
percent of the white residents are poor. In only one other census
tract does the percentage of poor whites exceed 10 percent (a level
of 14 percent poor whites in an area of Middle River). The ten
census tracts with the highest number of poor whites combine for
only about one-fifth of all the poor whites in the county.

[5]The cost-of-living index for metro Baltimore (110 percent) is higher than that for metro Indianapolis (94 percent). Adjusted for cost of living, a Baltimore Unigov's per capita income
($13,842) would be lower than Indianapolis Unigov's per capita income ($15,402), and Baltimore Unigov's poverty rate would be correspondingly higher (over 15 percent compared to
under 12 percent).

TABLE 3.3
Baltimore's poverty characteristics after a
hypothetical consolidation of Baltimore City and County

Community	Black Poverty, Population	Black Poverty, % of Black Population	White Poverty, Population	White Poverty, % of White Population
Baltimore City	118,177	28%	35,107	13%
Baltimore County	8,597	10%	27,041	5%
Consolidated City-County	126,774	24%	62,148	7%

By contrast, the ten census tracts with the highest number of poor blacks house one-half of Baltimore County's poor black population. In fact, even predominately middle class black suburbanites are substantially resegregated in Baltimore County. There are 15 census tracts with 50 percent or more black residents (while there are 100 census tracts that are 98 percent or more white). These 15 neighborhoods, primarily in Lochearn and Millford Mill, are home to 43 percent of all black residents of Baltimore County—and one-third of all poor blacks.

With a larger canvas on which to work, a consolidated government would have a much greater opportunity to pursue policies to open up a wider range of housing opportunities for poor blacks. A consolidated government could achieve greater socioeconomic integration throughout the 680-square-mile area than is being achieved now with the sharp jurisdictional split between Baltimore City and Baltimore County. Thus, there would be substantial benefits to consolidating the two jurisdictions.

However, while Baltimore City is clearly in decline, Baltimore County itself has barely grown in recent years. During the last decade, Baltimore County's population grew by only 36,000, or 5.4 percent. Baltimore County accounted for only 15 percent of the metro area's total population growth. Outlying areas in Harford County (16 percent), Anne Arundel County (24 percent), and Howard County (29 percent) accounted for the lion's share of new growth in the metro region. Such trends are projected to accelerate.

There is plenty of land within northern Baltimore County where new residential and commercial development could occur, but metro Baltimore is not expanding northward very much. The York, Pennsylvania, and Wilmington, Delaware, metro areas are not powerful economic growth centers, pulling the Baltimore area northward. The Washington, D.C. metro area is the great magnet. If anything, a healthy, dynamic Baltimore City would be an economic engine stimulating more vigorous development of northern Baltimore County.

Merging Baltimore City into Baltimore County now would not really recreate the Indianapolis Unigov of 1970—a community full of future potential. A consolidated Baltimore City-County would approximate the Indianapolis Unigov of 1995—a much sounder community than Baltimore City today but grappling with the fact that growth increasingly occurs outside its consolidated boundaries.

Merging Baltimore City with Baltimore County *and* Anne Arundel County would obviously substantially overcome these reservations. Frankly, as politically daunting as a Baltimore City–Baltimore County merger would be, the political hurdles to overcome in merging with Anne Arundel County (including Annapolis, Maryland's capital) would be so great that one might as usefully discuss one unitary government for the whole 2.4 million person Baltimore metropolitan area.

Merging Baltimore City into Baltimore County would be a major improvement over current conditions, but the optimum moment for that action passed by at least 20 years ago.

A Strategy That Will Work

1. Reducing Concentrated Poverty in Baltimore City through a Metropolitan Housing Strategy

Both annexation and consolidation have been rejected as strategies because they would not yield a canvas for action that includes new growth areas in metro Baltimore. Why are new communities important for the goal of relocating many of Baltimore City's poor?

One essential reason is geography. Poor people typically are more concentrated in hand-me-down neighborhoods. Heavily targeting rent subsidy programs on existing housing in closer-in, older neighborhoods, if anything, may accelerate the social and physical deterioration of such suburban neighborhoods.

The other reason is political. It has been the genius of Montgomery County's MPDU/HOC strategy to target communities *that are always in the process of being created.* There are no neighbors already in place in the proposed subdivision, townhouse project, or apartment complex who are organized to object. Moreover, by allocating 85 percent of new private housing construction to market rate housing, the MPDU/HOC policy requiring 10 percent affordable housing and 5 percent deep-subsidy housing is both a floor *and a ceiling.* Given market rate housing costs in metro Baltimore, new mixed-income developments are not likely to convert to low-income ghettoes over time.

A policy of promoting relocation of Baltimore City's low-income households would work best if the policy could be implemented significantly in new growth areas. The key, therefore, is to place the necessary planning, zoning, and housing assistance tools in some institutional framework to carry out such a long-term program.

The source of such authority most desirably would be the Maryland General Assembly, though it could occur through court order.[6] Such agreements are beyond the political ability (and often the statutory powers) of local elected officials. What would be the instrument for carrying it out?

We may reject out of hand the organization of one unitary "Metrogov" for the entire 2,609-square-mile, 2.4 million person area. The need for dramatically diminishing racial and economic segregation is acute, but that mission could get lost among the massive service delivery responsibilities of a unitary government. Reasonably effective local government on such a large scale is not unprecedented, but I would not wish upon the citizens of metro Baltimore the management and labor practices that have been perfected, for example, by New York City.

Can the metro area's seven counties (including Baltimore City) be entrusted independently to carry out such a metro-wide program? No! The Baltimore area's record of successful *voluntary* intergovernmental cooperation is relatively meager even on much less controversial issues such as regional transportation planning and regional water and sewage treatment. How much more difficult would voluntary cooperation be on an emotion-charged topic such as fair share low- and moderate-income housing? Even Montgomery County's exemplary program is, in effect, limited to low- and moderate-income families *who already live or work in Montgomery County.* By maintaining separate zoning controls, separate housing programs, and separate eligibility lists, a voluntary intergovernmental compact would produce minimal progress toward the essential goal: voluntary relocation of large numbers of poor black households from inner-city ghettos into nonpoor suburban communities.

Finally, though the authority for such a program desirably proceeds from state legislation, there are drawbacks to having the

---

[6]Federal and state courts have occasionally been the source of such policies. The most far-reaching example is the so-called Mt. Laurel decision of the New Jersey State Supreme Court. The issue of potential judicial action is discussed briefly in the Conclusion.

policy implemented through a state agency. (These are discussed below.)

2. Implementing a Comprehensive Planning, Zoning, and Housing Strategy by Forming a Metropolitan Municipality

The General Assembly should organize a Municipality of Metropolitan Baltimore, or "Metro" (following the example of state legislatures for Portland and Toronto). This would best fit metro Baltimore's circumstances. Metro's jurisdiction would cover Baltimore City and the six counties that currently comprise the Baltimore Metropolitan Statistical Area: Baltimore County and Anne Arundel, Carroll, Harford, Howard, and Queen Anne's Counties.

Metro would function as the upper tier of a two-tier system of local government. No existing government would be abolished. Metro's central mission would be to carry out metro-wide planning, zoning, and housing assistance programs, which are necessary to dissolve the high concentration of poverty in many Baltimore City neighborhoods. At the same time, Metro must protect suburban neighborhoods from becoming the next generation's slums, as is now occurring in so many older, inner suburbs around the country. "Balance, diversity, stability, everywhere" must be Metro's themes.

Metro would be governed by a Metropolitan Council, directly elected to represent the seven districts into which the metro area would be divided (again, examples are Portland and Toronto). It would be headed by a directly elected Metro Executive (Portland).

Metro would be endowed by the Maryland General Assembly with all the powers of any other municipality (and of any county, to the extent that counties have powers that are not available to municipalities). Metro's policy functions and public services would be assigned to it by the General Assembly, requested by local governments, or approved by vote of its constituents (as in Portland).

Metro's basic purpose, however, would not be to provide general public services but, as stated in its central mission, to mitigate patterns of urban development that create growing social inequities by race and income class.

The General Assembly would direct Metro to:

1. enact a regionwide Moderately-Priced Dwelling Unit ordinance (including the purchase of 5 percent of the units by the public housing authority) and monitor local governments' adherence to its provisions (Montgomery County);

2. establish a Metro-operated "Housing Opportunities Commission," which would:
   - absorb the assets, operations, and responsibilities of the various public housing agencies maintained by constituent governments to manage a regionwide public housing program (Metro Toronto);
   - assume the functions and responsibilities of the housing finance agencies of local governments or the State of Maryland for this jurisdictional area; and
   - establish a range of rental assistance and purchase programs for low- and moderate-income households throughout the regional area similar to the array of programs operated by Montgomery County;

3. establish a regionwide comprehensive land use plan in conjunction with local governments (Portland, Metro Toronto, Seattle);

4. as integral parts of the comprehensive plan, designate an urban growth boundary (Portland, Seattle) and set adequate public facilities requirements (Montgomery County, Metro Toronto) to bring about rational growth management and balance housing production with housing demand throughout the region;

5. monitor adherence of local government's plans, infrastructure investments, and zoning actions with the adopted general plan (Portland, Metro Toronto, King County);

6. serve as the Metropolitan Planning Organization for transportation planning within the region, including allocating federal funds under the Intermodal Surface Transportation Efficiency Act (Portland); and

7. establish a regionwide revenue sharing program (Metro Tax Base Pool) by pooling a portion of property tax base growth from commercial, industrial, and high-end residential property throughout the region (Twin Cities).

Metro's core administrative costs would be supported by a uniform property tax millage levied against all residential, commercial, and industrial property throughout its jurisdiction. This millage rate, including any ceiling, would be set forth in the authorizing legislation by the Maryland General Assembly (Portland).

Metro's housing programs would be supported by combining current federal and state grants with whatever portion of the Metro Tax Base Pool the Metro Council decides is necessary to achieve its housing goals.[7] For any other nonhousing activity, Metro could levy taxes for its operating budget and capital requirements as authorized by the General Assembly, by participating local governments, or by a majority of voters in its jurisdiction.

The remainder of this section will discuss Metro's geographic scope, its policy role, the Metro Council's composition, election of the executive, and the role of state government. The remaining sections will discuss the proposed fair share housing program and the tax base sharing program.

A. Geographic Scope

Urban America (even urban Canada) keeps spreading out. As was emphasized in Chapter Two, metropolitan areas keep expanding geographically decade by decade. Even the most ambitious attempts at metropolitan unification—Nashville, Jacksonville, Indianapolis, and Metro Toronto—experience significant population growth and economic activity leaping their boundaries as time passes. Within the 40-year study period, the definition of metropolitan Baltimore has grown from a three-jurisdiction area (Baltimore City, Baltimore County, Anne Arundel County) to a seven-jurisdiction area (adding Carroll, Harford, Howard, and Queen Anne's Counties). Other counties on Maryland's Eastern Shore will probably be added in future censuses.

Thus, Metro's jurisdictional area should be treated flexibly in the authorizing legislation. Metro's jurisdiction should be pegged to the definition of the Baltimore Metropolitan Statistical Area as defined by the Federal Office of Management and Budget (based on analyses conducted by the Bureau of the Census). This method of defining Metro's geographic coverage would allow for automatic expansion of Metro's jurisdiction, based on reasonably objective third-party analysis. By this mechanism, Metro's inclusion of new areas would not lag behind their incipient urbanization by too much time.

One exception to a possible future change in the Baltimore metro area's definition, however, ought to be made in the state authorizing legislation. Anne Arundel and Howard Counties should be permanently defined as part of Metro's jurisdiction even if a future federal decision might amputate those two counties from the Baltimore metro area to graft them onto the Washington metro area. Baltimore City (and, for that matter, Baltimore County)

---

[7]Given the imperative importance of the regionwide low-income housing strategies being proposed, using a portion of the annual revenues from the Metro Tax Base Pool will be essential.

should not be separated institutionally from the region's two highest-growth counties, nor should those two counties be provided an incentive to try to escape from Metro's jurisdiction through the doors of the federal Office of Management and Budget.

B. *Effective Policy Versus Efficient Services*

Proponents often try to justify governmental consolidation on the basis of greater efficiency, eliminating duplicative government programs, achieving economies of scale, and so on. *While it may be a beneficial result, greater efficiency is no part of this report's argument.* The most efficient scale for different services varies with the nature of the service. Sewage treatment, for example, is often best addressed at a regional level. Because of the high capital cost and technical complexities of sewage treatment facilities, there are truly economies of scale to be achieved. On the other hand, running neighborhood parks and manning local fire stations are services that are best provided on a small scale.

The current Baltimore region, like the rest of Maryland, is blessed with a system in which county governments are the primary local governments. The 2.4 million person Baltimore metro area has basically only 26 local governments—seven counties, including Baltimore City, and 19 municipalities (most with relatively limited functions).[8] In sharp contrast, the 2.3 million person Pittsburgh metro area has 330 local governments—five counties, 184 municipalities, and 141 townships!

Many public services are organized on a relatively efficient scale by county government. The smallest county (excluding Queen Anne's) is Carroll County (123, 372 residents). The largest is Baltimore City (736,014). Efficiency is generally a function of the quality of political leadership, the quality of professional management, and a skilled and motivated civil service. The most efficient local governments are generally found in medium-sized communities (i.e., between 100,000 and 750,000 residents), not in the 2.5 million population range that a unitary regional government for metro Baltimore would imply.

The Baltimore region suffers not from a failure of efficient public services but from the failure of effective public policy in dealing

---

[8]As was noted earlier, there are no municipalities in Baltimore County and only two in Anne Arundel County. Howard County also has no municipalities. Harford County has three, and Carroll County and Queen Anne's County have seven municipalities each. Only Aberdeen (13,087), Bel Air (8,860), and Havre de Grace (8,952) in Harford County and the City of Westminster (13,068) in Carroll County are of sufficient size to have major service delivery roles instead of their county government. Throughout the area, all public school systems are organized countywide.

with the impact of development patterns on social equity and opportunity. The proposed Metro would close the policy gap.

C. *Composition of the Metropolitan Council*

The Metropolitan Council would serve as the governing body of the new metro municipality. There are two reasons for the relatively small size of the proposed Metro Council (i.e., seven elected representatives). First, the area to be represented already has 2.4 million residents. To design council districts of a size in which candidates literally can campaign door-to-door (about 25,000–50,000 residents maximum) would require a legislative body of 50–100 members. Part-time state legislatures can function on such a scale; meeting on a weekly basis, local government cannot. Second, if we abandon the idea of districts scaled for door-to-door campaigning, what would be an effective size for the Metropolitan Council to function as a decision-making, policy-setting body? Having seven members seems to be about the size of many effective city councils, county commissions, and governing bodies of special governmental districts around the country.[9]

How should the council districts be drawn? The core issue is segregation by race and economic class, which already divide the region. Arranging districts by existing political jurisdictions may further divide the regional community and render Metro itself impotent.

By contrast, districts can be drawn as *bridges* unifying different segments of the metropolitan community. Therefore, the seven districts as proposed would provide each council member with a representative slice of the total metropolitan society.

As set forth in Table 3.4 and the accompanying Map 3.2, each of the proposed seven districts would be wedge-shaped. Each Metro Council district would

1. be formed by a block of contiguous census tracts;
2. contain a section of Baltimore City's downtown core (the regional center);
3. represent three or four counties (treating Baltimore City as one of seven counties);
4. include a portion of developing communities on the region's periphery;
5. be roughly equal in overall population, ranging from District 5 (306,458) to District 2 (383,462);

---

[9]Metro council members should be compensated at the same rate as Maryland county commissioners.

TABLE 3.4
Composition of proposed metro council districts

Community	Total Population	Black Population	% Black Population	Total Poverty Population	% Poverty Population	Per Capita Income
District 1	**344,126**	**76,574**	**22%**	**39,529**	**11%**	**$14,500**
Baltimore City	105,074	55,383	53%	28,597	27%	$9,957
Anne Arundel County	230,599	20,144	9%	9,902	4%	$16,618
Queen Anne's County	8,453	1,047	12%	1,030	12%	$13,204
District 2	**383,462**	**119,674**	**31%**	**34,747**	**9%**	**$13,803**
Baltimore City	104,543	81,936	78%	21,659	21%	$10,376
Anne Arundel County	212,995	31,757	15%	9,146	4%	$15,599
Baltimore County	64,652	5,981	9%	3,942	6%	$13,701
District 3	**356,169**	**143,102**	**40%**	**36,590**	**10%**	**$15,612**
Baltimore City	106,963	86,258	81%	26,147	24%	$11,666
Baltimore County	153,286	51,721	34%	7,900	5%	$17,651
Howard County	65,416	4,019	6%	1,840	3%	$16,794
Carroll County	31,776	1,104	3%	703	2%	$15,996
District 4	**362,305**	**69,881**	**19%**	**28,000**	**8%**	**$20,654**
Baltimore City	104,427	46,630	45%	19,298	18%	$19,771
Baltimore County	86,422	3,818	4%	3,619	4%	$22,741
Howard County	121,913	18,077	15%	3,944	3%	$21,981
Carroll County	49,543	1,356	3%	1,939	4%	$15,608
District 5	**306,458**	**84,281**	**28%**	**25,669**	**8%**	**$16,105**
Baltimore City	103,317	76,078	74%	17,219	17%	$12,067
Baltimore County	130,515	7,006	5%	5,170	4%	$19,249
Harford County	30,572	724	2%	1,394	5%	$17,475
Carroll County	42,053	473	1%	1,886	4%	$15,269
District 6	**339,632**	**59,855**	**18%**	**31,761**	**9%**	**$14,766**
Baltimore City	105,861	46,410	44%	19,333	18%	$12,502
Baltimore County	149,816	9,740	7%	9,590	6%	$15,373
Harford County	84,255	3,705	4%	2,838	3%	$16,478
District 7	**309,510**	**64,088**	**21%**	**39,089**	**13%**	**$13,580**
Baltimore City	105,919	43,073	41%	26,039	25%	$14,919
Baltimore County	110,757	7,122	6%	6,945	6%	$12,209
Queen Anne's County	25,500	2,792	11%	1,205	5%	$15,654
Harford County	67,334	11,101	16%	4,900	7%	$12,942

6. be as equal as possible in percentage of black residents (from District 6, with 18 percent, to District 3, with 40 percent);

7. be as equal as possible in percentage of poor population (from Districts 4 and 5, with 8 percent, to District 7, with 13 percent); and

8. fall within roughly the same per capita income range (from District 7, with $13,580, to District 4, with $20,654).

MAP 3.2
Baltimore Metropolitan Area by Metropolitan Council District
prepared by alan miller research/gis

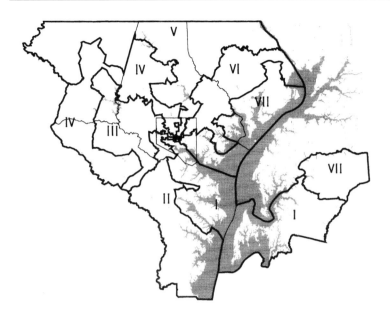

In addition, no county would be represented solely by one council member. Even Queen Anne's County, linked physically only by the Bay Bridge to the rest of the region, would be split between District 1 and District 7.

If these goals are accepted, more detailed computer analysis by census tract might produce some narrowing of these demographic ranges. However, it is impossible to equalize the districts for any of the criteria other than achieving near-perfect population balance among the districts. If the Baltimore region's current population were distributed in such a way as to yield equal proportions of blacks, poor people, income levels, and so on within the proposed districts, there would probably be no need for Metro at all!

Who would be elected to these Council seats? One hopes, as expressed above, that they would be individuals who are positively committed to Metro's mission. By the very nature of each district, the Metro Council members should share a sense of common constituency. Council members' background and community of residence must be left to the electoral process.

THE AQUARIUM WAS INTRODUCED INTO A FIRESTORM OF CONTROVERSY.

It Was Ultimately Approved by the Voters in 1976— But Not before Adversaries Deridingly Called It "The Mayor's Fish Tank."

In 1995, almost 20 years after it opened in 1976, the National Aquarium in Baltimore is reporting that on a busy, warm Sunday, it will host as many as 8,000 visitors.

Indeed, the aquarium's main problem is an enviable one: it could accommodate more fish-watchers, but at the more popular times it is already operating at capacity.

What a difference 19 years make!

The idea of the aquarium had been introduced to the community as early as 1973—into a firestorm of controversy. Finally, the bond issue (Question C) that would decide the aquarium's fate was put on the ballot in the 1976 election, for a vote by the electorate in the fall. For proponents and opponents, the summer leading up to that election was to be a long and hot one.

In June, the City Council approved the bill that put the issue on the ballot. Councilman Clarence "Du" Burns (D-2nd) was one of the proponents. "Somewhere along the line, we've got to make the decision on whether this city is going to move or stand still."

But Burns' councilmate Emerson Julian (D-4th) was just as adamantly against: "We're talking about a fish tank, that's what we're talking about."

As cold weather arrived, the controversy heated up. In September, Bettie Owings Summers, Co-chairman of the Baltimore City Coalition for Fair Taxation Assessments, took on the proponents in a stinging Op-Ed article. "We are puzzled by their rationale. The aquarium, they say, will bring conventions to Baltimore and conventions will create jobs. There are too many unproven assumptions in this thinking to convince us we can afford the luxury of the proposed aquarium."

But Arthur Liebeskind, chairman of the Baltimore City Aquarium Advisory Board, declared that the city couldn't afford not to build the aquarium. "It will stand in the tradition of Charles Center, the Inner Harbor, City Fair and Operation Sail—a vision of determination to revitalize a great city!" he said, adding praise for the project's biggest cheerleader, Mayor William Donald Schaefer.

As the election approached, both sides blanketed community associations and clubs with prop-

Continued on page 100

The issue of racial composition of the Metropolitan Council must be addressed directly. Arguments will be raised that the voting power of the black community is being diluted by enacting the Metro plan. Indeed, the proposed arrangement could be subject to challenge under the federal Voting Rights Act, which forbids drawing voting districts that decrease the likelihood of electing racial minorities to office.

According to this proposal, Baltimore City (which is now 60 percent black) would be split almost equally among seven different districts. In no district would blacks be in the majority (though the black proportion in District 3 would reach 40 percent). Does this represent disenfranchisement of the black population?

In my view, the major instrument of black disenfranchisement today is isolation of the black community, particularly of poor blacks. Some black political leaders (most notably Mayor Willie Herenton of Memphis, Tennessee) are now speaking out against such isolation.[10] By its very mission and the design of its districts, the Metro Council is intended to integrate the black community into the larger regional community.

Around the country, there are more and more examples of black political leaders successfully winning high office without dependence on a majority bloc of black votes. Mayor Norman Rice of Seattle, Mayor Wellington Webb of Denver, and Mayor Sharon Sayles Belton of Minneapolis are all black mayors of majority white cities. Are the voters of metro Baltimore less progressive racially than the voters of Seattle, Denver, and Minneapolis?

Drawing up the Metro Council's districts is certainly a topic on which political compromises will be hammered out if any such plan is ever to be enacted by the Maryland General Assembly. One compromise alternative would be to use cumulative voting for the election of Metro Council members. One resident could be elected from each district through an at-large election in which all seven council members would be elected by all the registered voters in the Metro area. Each voter would be allowed to cast up to seven votes and could cumulate his or her votes for one or more chosen candidates. Winning candidates would be the top vote-getters from each district. Black voters (or any other interest

---

[10]Noting the rapid isolation of the City of Memphis, Mayor Herenton, the city's first black mayor, reinstituted a policy of annexation. (Annexations by Memphis had ceased around 1980.) After fierce resistance by predominantly white suburbs, in 1993 the mayor proposed "dissolving" the city of Memphis and having surrounding Shelby County become, in effect, a unitary, near-metropolitan government for both Memphis and its suburbs. The mayor's proposal was bitterly attacked by both white and black critics. However, it would be a bold and effective way to reenergize the Memphis area, which seems to fall just short of achieving critical mass in its fight for recognition as a "big league" community.

The Aquarium Was Introduced into a Firestorm of Controversy.
(continued)

aganda. City Council President Walter S. Orlinsky joined the opponents who had been calling the aquarium "the mayor's fish tank."

The vote was close. Early returns on Nov. 2, 1976 had the "fors" trailing by as many as 1,500 votes. But support for the "Mayor's fish tank" gained momentum as the night wore on. The "for" in Question C passed by some 18,000 votes.

Today, in 1995, in terms of paid visitors, it is high among the state's largest tourist attractions.

Once again, to get to where it was going, Baltimore chose to swim against the current.

---

group, e.g., environmentalists, farmers) could give as many of their respective seven votes—even all of them—to their preferred candidates, increasing the chances of representation by at least one favored candidate.

In my view, cumulative voting could create almost as divisive and parochial a Metro Council as one elected by traditional city and county jurisdictions. It could result in a Metro Council composed of the environmentalists' representative, the farmers' representative, and so on. However, cumulative voting is hardly un-American. It is used in local elections in Peoria, Illinois; Cambridge, Massachusetts; Alamogordo, New Mexico; and several Alabama counties. At the direction of a federal judge, cumulative voting may be instituted in local elections in Maryland's own Worcester County. These are matters to be dealt with through Maryland's own political institutions.

D. *Election of the Metro Executive*

The executive officer of Portland Metro is the only directly elected chief executive of a regional organization in the United States. (The Chairman of Metro Toronto has also been directly elected since 1988.) Why does this report recommend an elected Metro Executive rather than an appointed executive officer who is then accountable to the Metropolitan Council?

First, I have a preference for an elected chief executive based on my own experience as mayor of Albuquerque. My personal preference coincides with citizen preferences throughout much of the state of Maryland. Maryland voters have opted for the strong mayor-council form of government for its principal city (Baltimore City) or the elected county executive–county council form of government for many of its major counties, such as Baltimore County, Montgomery County, and Prince George's County.[11]

Second, it is hoped that the nature of Metro's council districts would produce council members with a sense of broad constituency who would overcome more parochial, jurisdictional interests. However, a Metro Executive elected regionwide would truly have a regional constituency.

Third, above all, Metro must be animated by a sense of vision. It is difficult to develop vision by committee, despite all the "visioning" processes being conducted in communities around the country. In public life, uplifting visions typically come together in the mind and soul of a political leader who can then rally others around that vision. To succeed, Metro will need the kind of visionary leadership that Frederick Gardiner provided as the founding chairman of Metro Toronto or the political drive that Richard Lugar and William Hudnut brought to bear on the problems of Indianapolis–Marion County.

E. The Role of State Government

Why cannot just setting up another state agency achieve the goals set forth for Metro? Metro cannot come into existence without decisive but controversial action by the Maryland General Assembly and the governor. Why shouldn't the state's political leadership choose to vest responsibility for implementing these policies in a state agency organized for the task?

First, in many respects, the shortcomings of having a state agency in that role are already apparent. The Metropolitan Council of the Twin Cities area is, in effect, a state agency. Its 17 members are appointed by the governor and confirmed by the state senate. Its employees are state employees. During its 28-year existence, its spirit has become largely bureaucratic. Its fortunes rest, in substantial measure, on the interests and commitments of whoever is governor of Minnesota. In its early years, activist, progressive governors named activist, progressive ap-

---

[11]Following the parallel established above, the Metro Executive ought to be compensated on a scale equivalent to that of such county executives.

pointees to the Metropolitan Council. Over the last three gubernatorial administrations, Minnesota has had more conservative governors who were generally unenthusiastic about (if not, in one past instance, even inimical to) the Metropolitan Council's mission. On the whole, recent appointees to the Metropolitan Council have not acted with the passion and conviction of the Council's earlier members, and the Metropolitan Council has languished. In the long run, it is better to rely on the electoral process.

Second, state government has statewide responsibilities and cannot focus solely on metro Baltimore. The health and vitality of metropolitan Baltimore must always be one of the state's primary concerns, since the Baltimore metro area is Maryland's primary population and economic center. However, the Baltimore metro area has only half of the state's population. Montgomery County and Prince Georges County are the state's two most populous counties (and Montgomery County is the wealthiest). The Washington metro area is rapidly expanding into southern Maryland. Both the Eastern Shore and Western Maryland have problems and interests that are different from those of the Baltimore region. The governor and the General Assembly cannot devote the attention and energy that are required to accomplish Metro's mission and still attend to the interests of the rest of the state. A Metro Council could do so.

Third, though housing and development policy must be Metro's focus, it would have a broad array of policy responsibilities and, potentially, service delivery responsibilities. Metro would not be one-dimensional, as most state agencies are. The scope and complexity of Metro's task would require clear and direct accountability for performance. Within the political and bureaucratic structure of current state government, such accountability could be obscured. Having set the organization in motion, the governor and General Assembly should step back and let Metro do its job.

The governor and the General Assembly could ease Metro's job by legislating MPDU-type requirements for all jurisdictions statewide.[12] Such a state law should provide some local flexibility to meet local conditions. (For example, the smaller scale of development projects in many counties might make Montgomery County's 50-unit minimum inappropriate statewide, or 50 units may be less aggressive than others may want.) However, a uniform

---

[12]In the 22 years since Montgomery County's pioneering action, only Prince George's County has adopted a similar policy recently. The Howard County Council rejected such a proposal.

state law would simplify the Metro Council's political task. It would also be good policy for any community.

3. Measuring the Impact of the Housing Recommendations

The following sections will address the projected demographic, social, economic, and fiscal impacts of carrying through the housing recommendations sketched out in previous sections. I will introduce evidence from other communities' experiences to support the projections. Initially, I will offer some goals for the Baltimore region, and outline the kinds of changes in population and housing trends that would be necessary to accomplish these goals. The reader is asked to suspend critical judgment based on conventional views of political realities. First let's find out what the actual numbers would be to reach these goals; then let's assess how difficult it would be to achieve them.

A. Goals for a Metro Housing Program

The central mission of a Municipality of Metropolitan Baltimore, guided by an elected Metro Council and an elected Metro Executive, would be to open up housing choices for Baltimore City's poor black households to allow them to relocate more evenly throughout the region. This would require a comprehensive set of planning, zoning, and housing policies that Metro would be empowered to carry out by state law. To set goals for such a metro-wide housing policy, we must examine more thoroughly the geography of poverty in the Baltimore region.

The overall level of poverty throughout the Baltimore region is not the central issue. Over the past two decades, the region's economy has performed well (see Chapter One). Despite the continuing loss of manufacturing jobs, particularly toward the end of the 1970s, the region's overall poverty rate actually declined from 11.3 percent in 1969 to 10.1 percent in 1989—somewhat below the national urban average. The issue is the *concentration of poverty* by political jurisdiction, neighborhood, and race.

Table 3.5 summarizes poverty trends by political jurisdiction. Over the past two decades, while the regional poverty rate dropped, the poverty rate increased in Baltimore City from 18.4 percent to 21.9 percent. By contrast, poverty rates fell in all suburban counties except Baltimore County. As new, middle class subdivisions sprang up in the outlying counties, the number of poorer households in traditional rural communities and small towns

TABLE 3.5
While the regional poverty rate fell, Baltimore
City's poverty level increased (1970–1990)

City or County	Poverty Rate, 1970	Poverty Rate, 1990	Fair Share of Poverty Index, 1970	Fair Share of Poverty Index, 1990
Metro Baltimore	**11.3%**	**10.1%**	**100**	**100**
Baltimore City	18.4%	21.9%	163	217
Anne Arundel County	7.1%	4.5%	63	45
Baltimore County	4.5%	5.5%	40	54
Carroll County	8.6%	3.8%	76	38
Harford County	7.7%	5.1%	68	50
Howard County	5.2%	3.1%	46	31
Queen Anne's County	N/A	6.7%	N/A	66

shrank in relative importance. Some poorer, long-time residents may even have been squeezed out of their former communities and into the city by rising land and housing costs and escalating property taxes.

Measuring changes in each jurisdiction's fair share of poverty index illustrates contrasting trends.[13] In 20 years, Baltimore City's fair share of poverty index moved upward from a moderate 163 to a stressful 217—in other words, Baltimore City has more than twice its fair share of the region's poor. With poverty increasing as well in older, inner suburbs such as Essex, Dundalk, and Lansdowne–Baltimore Highlands, Baltimore County's fair share of poverty index edged upward (from 40 to 54). On the other hand, the other counties' fair share of poverty indices all fell: Anne Arundel (63 to 45), Carroll (76 to 38), Harford (68 to 50), Howard (46 to 31), and, most probably, Queen Anne's as well. The Baltimore region is becoming more and more differentiated by income class among its various jurisdictions. Baltimore City has more than twice its fair share of the region's poor, and its poverty burden is rising. The suburban counties have about half their fair shares, and, except for Baltimore County, their incidence of poverty is falling countywide.

What are the dynamics of poverty at the neighborhood level? It is common to characterize census tracts where between 20 percent and 40 percent of the residents are poor as "poverty neighbor-

---

[13]As was discussed in Chapter One, the fair share of poverty index is simply the ratio between the percentage of poverty regionwide and the percentage of poverty in a given local jurisdiction. "Fair share" equals "100." Above 100, a jurisdiction has more than its proportionate share of poor residents. Below 100, a jurisdiction has less than its proportionate share.

TABLE 3.6
Almost all poor neighborhoods (92 of 103) are in Baltimore City;
almost half of city neighborhoods are poor (1990)

City or County	Total Census Tracts	Poverty Census Tracts (20–40% Poor)	High-Poverty Census Tracts (40–60% Poor)	Hyper-Poverty Census Tracts (60–100% Poor)
Metro Baltimore	721	65	33	5
Baltimore City	203	57	30	5
Anne Arundel County	124	2	2	0
Baltimore County	245	4	0	0
Carroll County	29	1	0	0
Harford County	62	1	1	0
Howard County	47	0	0	0
Queen Anne's County	11	0	0	0

hoods." Census tracts where 40–60 percent of the residents are poor are characterized as "high-poverty neighborhoods," and census tracts where poverty exceeds 60 percent of the residents are "hyper-poverty neighborhoods."

Table 3.6 shows that in 1990, the region's poorer neighborhoods were highly concentrated within Baltimore City, which had 92 of the region's 103 poor neighborhoods. Substantial poverty characterized almost half of Baltimore City's 203 census tracts. Indeed, in 35 census tracts—over one-sixth of all city neighborhoods—over 40 percent of the residents are poor (and in five of these, poverty levels exceed 60 percent).

The suburban picture is dramatically different. Of 518 suburban census tracts across the six counties, in only nine are 20 percent or more of the residents poor, and in only three poor neighborhoods (two located in Annapolis) do poverty levels exceed 40 percent.

Poverty has been spreading geographically within Baltimore City over these two decades. As Table 3.7 shows, between 1970 and 1990, the total number of poverty neighborhoods increased from 70 to 90.[14] During that 20-year period, the poverty level had increased substantially in 30 city census tracts, remained relatively stable in 32 tracts, and declined in only eight. However, in only one of those eight census tracts did poverty decline sufficiently to drop the neighborhood below the 20 percent

---

[14]By the 1990 census, two additional census tracts had been separately designated, having been created out of larger tracts in the 1970 census.

TABLE 3.7
The number of poverty neighborhoods has spread within Baltimore City

Category	1970	1990
Poverty neighborhoods (20–40% poor)	47	63
High-poverty neighborhoods (40–60% poor)	21	29
Hyper-poverty neighborhoods (more than 60% poor)	2	4
Total	70	90

threshold—and just barely at that.[15] In effect, in racially segregated housing markets like the Baltimore region, ghettos only become bigger ghettos.

Poverty neighborhoods are also developing in some older suburbs. In 1970, there were only three such neighborhoods (two in the city of Annapolis, one in the Dundalk area of Baltimore County). By 1990, the list of suburban poverty neighborhoods had grown to 11 with a block of depressed neighborhoods having emerged in the Essex area of Baltimore County.

How does poverty impact the Baltimore region by race? The 1990 census counted 90,187 poor whites and 137,441 poor blacks in the Baltimore region—roughly two poor whites for every three poor blacks. However, the overall poverty level among whites (5 percent) is dramatically lower than that among blacks (23 percent).

Table 3.8 underscores the sharply different circumstances of black city residents and black suburban residents. Whereas 28 percent of all city blacks are poor, poverty among suburban blacks ranges from only 7 percent (in Howard County) to 13 percent in Harford County. (Though now part of the Baltimore region, Queen Anne's County still has a substantial rural—and poorer—sector of its population.) Overwhelmingly, suburban blacks constitute a solidly middle class population. Moreover, many middle class blacks still live in city neighborhoods where poverty levels are high and increasing. Sixty percent of all blacks in Baltimore City live in poverty neighborhoods—over 20 percent of all city blacks live in neighborhoods of high or hyper poverty. As neighborhood conditions deteriorate, more and more middle class blacks are

[15]In census tract 2201, the poverty level dropped from 33.3 percent (1970) to 19.9 percent (1990).

TABLE 3.8
Black poverty rates are generally two to three times higher
than white poverty rates throughout the metro area

City or County	% White Residents in Poverty	% Black Residents in Poverty
Metro Baltimore	5.4%	23.2%
Baltimore City	12.6%	27.9%
Anne Arundel County	3.3%	13.6%
Annapolis City	5.4%	25.3%
Baltimore County	4.7%	10.4%
Carroll County	3.6%	12.3%
Harford County	4.3%	14.1%
Howard County	2.5%	7.3%
Queen Anne's County	5.1%	19.9%

moving from the city to suburban neighborhoods, where there are better housing buys, better schools, safer neighborhoods.

The net result is that 86 percent of all poor blacks in the Baltimore region live in Baltimore City (Table 3.9). Almost three-quarters (72 percent) of poor blacks live in poor neighborhoods, and 32 percent of poor blacks live in high- or hyper-poverty neighborhoods where the poverty level exceeds 40 percent.

The substantial suburbanization of poor whites has created an entirely different social environment for them. Though there are over 90,000 poor whites in the Baltimore region, few live in poverty neighborhoods. Only 24 percent of all poor whites live in poverty

TABLE 3.9
While 59% of all poor whites live in the suburbs,
86% of poor blacks live in Baltimore City

City or County	% of Metro Area's Poor Whites by Community	% of Metro Area's Poor Blacks by Community
Metro Baltimore	**100%**	**100%**
Baltimore City	41%	86%
Anne Arundel County	12%	4%
Baltimore County	30%	6%
Carroll County	5%	0.2%
Harford County	7%	2%
Howard County	4%	1%
Queen Anne's County	2%	0.5%

neighborhoods, and only 5 percent of poor whites live in high-poverty neighborhoods.

For white area residents of all income levels, living in poverty conditions is very rare; fewer than 5 percent of all whites live in poverty neighborhoods, and fewer than 1 percent of all whites live in high-poverty neighborhoods. By contrast, 43 percent of all blacks (of whatever income level) live in poverty neighborhoods, and 15 percent of all blacks live in high-poverty neighborhoods.

Being poor is personally hard for any household, regardless of race. But living in whole neighborhoods of *concentrated* poverty is a curse that affects almost entirely only black residents—both poor and middle class blacks.

There are many today who argue that segregation in urban America is really just the result of differences in economic class. How would those who assert that argument answer the most striking findings of the previous sections?

Three out of every four people who are poor and *white* live in nonpoor, or middle class neighborhoods in the Baltimore region.

Three out of every four people who are poor and black live in poor neighborhoods in Baltimore City.

The initial goal of Metro's housing policies would be to assist poor blacks to achieve the same general pattern of widespread dispersion that now benefits poor whites in metro Baltimore.

This goal does not mean that poor blacks would be encouraged to move into neighborhoods that already have a substantial proportion of poor whites. Nobody's interest is served (including the families that are moving) by increasing current concentrations of poor households of whatever race or ethnicity in any neighborhood. The intent is to achieve for poor black households the same general assimilation into middle class neighborhoods that poor white households already experience in the Baltimore region.

B. Scope of a Metro Housing Program

To assess the actual number of housing units required, the analysis will now shift from focusing on "persons" to focusing on "households." As Table 3.10 illustrates, the distribution of households is virtually identical to the distribution of persons.

In this section, I'll examine two ways of illustrating hypothetical goals for a regionwide, dispersed low-income housing program for inner-city residents. The first method will assume that poor blacks would be living in each county in the same proportions as poor whites. It also assumes that there would be no reduction in poverty

TABLE 3.10

Current and hypothetical distribution of black households
compared to poor white households by city and county

City or County	Share of Metro Poor White Households	Poor Black Households, Current Distribution	Poor Blacks Distributed as Poor White Households	Poor Black Households as % of All Households
Metro Baltimore	100%	47,331	47,331	5%
Baltimore City	41%	40,541	19,211	7%
Anne Arundel County	12%	2,104	5,538	4%
Baltimore County	30%	2,979	14,325	5%
Carroll County	5%	124	2,247	5%
Harford County	7%	686	3,377	5%
Howard County	4%	578	1,837	3%
Queen Anne's County	2%	319	795	6%

as a result of reducing the high concentration of inner-city poverty. This illustration will be covered in Tables 3.10–3.14.

Though better than current conditions, that would not be a truly balanced, regionwide approach. Baltimore County is already home to a large proportion (30 percent) of the metro area's poor whites. While the fair share of poverty index has been falling in all other suburban counties, Baltimore County's index has been rising over the past 20 years. A more equitable regional program would take into account both Baltimore County's growing vulnerability and the probability that successfully deconcentrating inner-city poverty would result in more people escaping poverty itself. An alternative approach is illustrated in Tables 3.15 and 3.16.

If poor black households were distributed throughout the metro area as poor white households currently are, the number of poor black households within Baltimore City would be cut in half (from 40,541 to 19,211). There would be corresponding increases of poor black households in Baltimore's suburbs. The proportional increases look large. For example, the number of poor black households would more than double in Anne Arundel and Queen Anne's Counties, more than triple in Howard County, and increase almost fivefold in Baltimore County. However, such relative increases in poor black households would really reflect the current degree of racial exclusion within those counties. To repeat, under this proposed goal, this hypothetical distribution of poor black households in suburban areas would only match the distribution of poor white families in the same counties.

Even after such a redistribution, the proportion of poor black households within the total population of suburban communities would be modest. Poor black households as a percentage of total population would range from only 3 percent of Howard County to 6 percent of Queen Anne's County. In the process, the proportion of poor black households within Baltimore City would drop from 14 percent to slightly over 7 percent.

Turning to the housing market, Table 3.11 identifies the number of low-cost housing units within the metro area. For these purposes, low-cost housing units are defined as rental units that, in 1990, did not exceed $400 per month gross rent (including utilities) and owner-occupied homes that, in 1990, did not exceed $400 per month in mortgage costs and utilities. At the maximum rental or home ownership costs, $400 per month would represent about 38 percent of the gross income of a poor family of four at the poverty threshold (defined as $12,674 in 1989).

What is notable about this comparison is that each suburban jurisdiction already has about twice the number of low-cost housing units that would be required by the proposed relocation of 21,000 poor black households from Baltimore City to the suburbs. That, of course, does not mean that such units are standing vacant, awaiting their new residents. Most are already occupied, mostly by poor white families. Others are already occupied by poorer black suburbanites or by other people (black or white) who are *not* poor.

Moreover, it would not be desirable either merely to supplant poor white households with poor black households in the same housing nor to have the proportion of poor households grow significantly within the same apartment complexes or neighborhoods. Nothing is gained by shrinking poor black ghettos within Baltimore City and recreating new economic ghettos—either black or

TABLE 3.11

The number of housing units needed under the new housing program compared to the number currently available by city and county

City or County	Current No. of Low-Cost Homes	Current No. of Low-Cost Rentals	No. of Housing Units Needed for Poor Blacks
Metro Baltimore	**26,978**	**92,814**	**N/A**
Baltimore City	11,053	64,650	−21,329
Anne Arundel County	4,081	5,536	3,434
Baltimore County	8,034	14,141	11,346
Carroll County	1,111	2,368	2,123
Harford County	1,745	3,910	2,691
Howard County	527	1,531	1,259
Queen Anne's County	427	678	476

TABLE 3.12
New housing starts in Baltimore, 1970–1989

City or County	New Housing Units, 1970–1979	New Housing Units, 1980–1989
Metro Baltimore	171,068	173,384
Baltimore City	23,123	16,171
Anne Arundel County	41,072	37,829
Baltimore County	52,296	47,787
Carroll County	11,467	13,681
Harford County	16,948	20,180
Howard County	22,656	33,117
Queen Anne's County	3,506	4,629

integrated—in the suburbs. This is, indeed, the typical fate of older, inner-ring suburbs around inelastic central cities—and is the pattern already evident in the Baltimore region. As was discussed earlier, in 11 suburban census tracts, 20 percent or more of the black residents are poor; almost all such tracts are in older neighborhoods closer in to the Baltimore City limits (or in older but nonhistoric sections of Annapolis).

Some of the existing stock of low-income housing can be used to achieve the proposed goal of more even relocation of poor black families throughout the metro area. However, great care must be exercised to not allow older suburban neighborhoods to become overly impacted. *New* housing in *new* neighborhoods must play a substantial role in the overall strategy.

What is the potential for new housing to contribute to the solution? Table 3.12 summarizes new housing starts for the Baltimore region from 1970 to 1989. We might project that about 20,000 new housing units a year will be built in the Baltimore region over the next 20 years.[16] What if, through the proposed Metro, a Montgomery County–type Moderately-Priced Dwelling Unit policy were established? In short, in all new developments of 50 or more units (whether single-family homes, townhouses, or apartments), a total of 15 percent of all units would have to be devoted to below-market-price affordable housing. Furthermore, the Metro Coun-

---

[16]The number of new housing units authorized for construction in the Baltimore metro area averaged slightly over 13,000 units per year from 1990 to 1993. This period covered one of the deepest downturns in the housing industry in decades, so there is reason to believe that housing starts will rise toward the 20,000 per year level. Obviously, if annual housing starts continued to average 13,000 for the next 20 years, the following projections would be reduced by one-third. The gap would have to be made up in greater purchase or rental of existing housing in existing neighborhoods.

THE HISTORY OF THE MECHANIC THEATER
Is the History of the Community's Trying to Get It Right. It Opened Then Closed Then Opened Again! "Hey! I can SEE from My Seat!"

The area in front of the Mechanic Theater on the night of Nov. 1, 1976 was all klieg lights and TV cameras and microphones propping up everywhere; furred and bejeweled ladies; tuxedoed men. And the night itself was invested with the glitter and glamour and magic that go with the comings and goings of celebrities.

It was not, as you might have thought, "Opening Night" at the Mechanic; that had been nine years earlier. (Betty Grable starred in "Hello Dolly.") For the Mechanic, those nine years contained all of the elements of a Broadway play fit for the stage of the Mechanic itself—disappointment, hope, success, failure, dreams, faith, love and in the end, the triumph of light over darkness.

But first, for your better understanding of this play, some program notes: Baltimore's legitimate theater until 1964 (when it was razed) had been Ford's Theater, owned by Morris Mechanic, on Fayette Street between Eutaw and Howard. (It is now a parking lot.) Some of the shows that would have played Ford's played, instead, at Painter's Mill Music Fair, and for one season, at the Old Stanley (later the Stanton) Theater at Howard and Centre (now a parking lot). But the arrangement failed to draw support, and Mr. Mechanic announced that he would build a new legitimate theater as part of Charles Center.

He did, and hopes were high as the curtain went up that opening night of Jan. 16, 1967. But a funny thing happened when the curtain went down. Some people were whispering to one another, even as they were politely applauding, that they couldn't hear (or in some cases, couldn't see) what was said or sung, or who was doing the saying or the singing. The reviews for "Hello Dolly" were pretty good, but for the Mechanic itself they were not. People wondered if Baltimore's new showcase of a legitimate theater had bombed.

Nonetheless, show business being show business, the Mechanic went bravely on. One reason was that the theater had been leased to the James Nederlander Corp. of New York on a ten year lease. Subscriptions reached 18,000, one of the highest in the country. But problems plagued the Mechanic; the audience dwindled, and Neder-

Continued on page 114

cil's own "Housing Opportunities Commission" would be directed and financed to buy one-third of the affordable units, or 5 percent of the total supply of new housing, as deep-subsidy rentals for low-income households.

It is important to account for the proportion of housing starts to which the MPDU policy would not apply—that is, individual custom-built housing or speculative homes or homes built within single-family or multifamily developments of fewer than 50 units. On the basis of Montgomery County's experience, approximately half of all housing starts occur in projects of 50 or more units that fall within the MPDU requirements. In short, we might anticipate that about 10,000 housing units a year would be built at a project scale to which the policy would apply.

Table 3.13 projects what the impact of such a program might be.

Of the 10,000 new units produced per year in projects to which the MPDU policy would apply, about 1,000 (10 percent) would be required to be affordable housing that would be within the purchase or rental range of households earning a maximum of 80 percent of the Baltimore region's median household income. Another 500 (5 percent) per year would be acquired by the Metro Council's Housing Opportunities Commission as deep-subsidy units for public housing eligible households. It is these units that would be systematically used as the primary housing resource to meet the goal of voluntarily relocating 21,000 poor black households from Baltimore City. Over a 20-year period, these would amount to about 10,000 homes and apartments, enough to absorb about half of the 21,000 poor black households being voluntarily relocated

TABLE 3.13

Proposed new annual housing starts and number of units dedicated to affordable and low-income households under proposed MPDU program for Baltimore

City or County	Annual New Housing Units	Annual New Affordable Units (10%)	Annual New HOC-Bought Units (5%)
Metro Baltimore	**10,000**	**1,000**	**500**
Baltimore City	600	60	30
Anne Arundel County	2,200	220	110
Baltimore County	2,500	250	125
Carroll County	800	80	40
Harford County	1,400	140	70
Howard County	2,200	220	110
Queen Anne's County	300	30	15

THE HISTORY OF THE MECHANIC THEATER
(continued)

lander advised the city that he would either break the lease or turn the Mechanic into a movie theater. (The erratic opening and closing of the Charcoal Hearth within the theater complex did not help.) Enter from off-stage: Mayor Schaefer and the downtown merchants. Here the story line is enlivened.

Three leading citizens were organized as Baltimore Theater, Inc. to take over. They were Howard Owen, married to Mr. Mechanic's niece; Jack Fruchtman, owner of the New Theater, among other theaters, and Frank Roberts, a sports promoter. In two years they called it curtains.

The Mechanic stayed dark for 18 months.

Now enter the City of Baltimore with half a million dollars in improvements. With the assist of a 20 year lease from the Mechanic, and the retention of New York impresario Alex Cohen, things began to happen.

Walls were moved inward, the orchestra pit was doubled in size and acoustical improvements were made throughout. (The new management also brought back the Charcoal Hearth restaurant under the name of Cafe Des Artistes.)

Which brings us to "Opening Night" of the "new" Mechanic, Nov. 1, 1976 and the klieg lights and the diamonds and the furs and the celebrities. The show was "The Sly Fox," featuring George C. Scott, and the audience was free and ready with its critique for the new Mechanic. "It's smaller, but I can see from my seat for a change," one patron told a roving reporter. Another: "Hey, they got steps; no more clunking down the old ramp!"

So on this second "Opening Night" not only did the critics like the show, the audience liked the Mechanic. Baltimore had waited nine years for it.

And in 1995 the Mechanic, happily, is still playing the best of Broadway.

In the end, the story of the Mechanic was a typical Baltimore performance; to make it happen it took lots of practice, practice, practice.

(Table 3.14). The HOC's share of new housing would cover about half to two-thirds of the relocation targets in Anne Arundel, Carroll, Harford, and Queen Anne's Counties over the 20-year period.

New housing construction would cover only one-quarter of the relocation target for Baltimore County. As the oldest and most

TABLE 3.14
The number of units needed from existing housing to meet MPDU
program requirements for Baltimore at 10% poverty level

City or County	20 Years of New Low Income Units	Relocated Poor Black Households	Units Needed from Existing Housing
Baltimore MSA	10,000	21,329	11,329
Baltimore City	600	N/A	N/A
Anne Arundel County	2,200	3,434	1,234
Baltimore County	2,500	11,346	8,846
Carroll County	800	2,123	1,323
Harford County	1,400	2,691	1,291
Howard County	2,200	1,259	–941
Queen Anne's County	300	476	176

built-out of Baltimore City's suburbs, the rate of new construction in Baltimore County is proportionally less than in the newer, outer suburbs. However, equally relevant to our goals is the fact that Baltimore County is the home to a large number of poor white households. In this example, because its projected share of poor black households would be based on its proportion of poor white households, Baltimore County would have the highest target to meet. (In the following section, we will discuss a more "fair share" approach that would reduce Baltimore County's target for resettled poor black households.)

Howard County contrasts strikingly with Baltimore County. Howard County is the area's fastest-growing county, and new construction is high. The projection of MPDU-related units for Howard County would yield a total number of HOC-owned units that is almost twice Howard County's projected target for relocated households. However, Howard County has substantially less than its fair share of poor households (white as well as black). It is appropriate that an expanded HOC-owned housing supply would be available to allow the increase of low-income residents to a level more approximating Howard County's "fair share."

What if, for reasons discussed below, the level of poverty metrowide were reduced from the current level of 10 percent to a future level of 8 percent as a result of integrating a large proportion of the poor black population into suburban middle class communities? If the goal for all suburban counties was to have a fair share of poor households—for instance, a share equal to 6.5 percent of each county's total population—the balance of poor households would continue to live in Baltimore City. The city's proportion of poor households (white and black) would fall from the current level of 21 percent to 11.5 percent. The results of redistribution are shown in Table 3.15. Comparing suburban counties' "relocated poor black households" at the reduced level of poverty overall with the similar calculation in Table 3.14, the number of poor black households projected for Carroll, Harford, and Queen Anne's Counties would be reduced by 33 to 50 percent. With its relatively high proportion of poor white households, Baltimore County's fair share of poor black households would be reduced from 11,346 to 4,163. Anne Arundel County's target would increase slightly from 3,434 households to 3,872 households. Howard County would experience a greater increase in its target fair share (from 1,259 to 2,397). However, attaining its fair share would still leave Howard County with poor black households representing 4.6 percent of its total population.

Measuring the proposed regional MPDU program against the anticipated lower poverty level, Table 3.16 shows that each suburban county would satisfy at least 60 percent of its fair share target of poor black households through new housing construction. Few existing single-family neighborhoods and apartment complexes would need to participate in the program in a major way.

For the previous pages (and 16 statistical tables), the reader has been asked to suspend judgment while I've tried to show the nature and scope of the potential solution. The problem is the high concentration of poor black households within Baltimore City. (As was noted, poor white households are much more highly dispersed through the metro area.) The key to the solution is to create a

TABLE 3.15
Distribution of poor black households by city and county under proposed MPDU fair share program at 8% metro-wide poverty level

City or County	All Poor as % of Population 8%/ Fair Share	Net Relocated Poor Black Households at 8% Poverty	Total Poor Black Households at 8% Poverty	Black Poor as % of Population 8%/ Fair Share
Metro Baltimore	**8.0%**	**−9,547**	**37,784**	**4.6%**
Baltimore City	11.4%	−22,607	17,934	7.1%
Anne Arundel County	6.5%	3,872	5,976	4.1%
Baltimore County	6.5%	4,163	7,142	3.0%
Carroll County	6.5%	1,347	1,471	3.5%
Harford County	6.5%	1,319	2,005	3.2%
Howard County	6.5%	2,397	2,975	4.6%
Queen Anne's County	6.5%	330	649	5.5%

TABLE 3.16
The number of units needed from existing housing to meet MPDU
program requirements for Baltimore at 8% poverty level

City or County	20 Years of New Low Income Units	Relocated Poor Black Households 8% Poverty	Additional Units from Existing Housing
Baltimore MSA	10,000	13,060	3,060
Baltimore City	600	N/A	N/A
Anne Arundel County	2,200	3,872	1,672
Baltimore County	2,500	4,163	1,663
Carroll County	880	1,347	547
Harford County	1,400	1,319	−81
Howard County	2,200	2,397	197
Queen Anne's County	300	330	30

greater range of housing types in new construction in Baltimore
suburbs through a Montgomery County–type MPDU/HOC policy administered by the proposed Metro government. Through
systematic actions to allow voluntary relocation of poor black
households into new, scattered site, suburban housing, over the
next two decades the incidence of poverty within Baltimore City
would be cut in half while the proportion of poor people (black
and white) within each suburban county would not exceed 6.5
percent, which would still be below the projected regional average
poverty rate of 8 percent.

How could the program be managed to significantly benefit
poor black households within Baltimore City when there are so
many poor white households in metro Baltimore? Poor white
households have a significant need for housing assistance as well.
Would not the Metro Housing Opportunities Commission have to
operate its programs in an evenhanded, color-blind manner?

The answer is obviously "yes," but the very organization of a *regionwide* housing agency and *regionwide* eligibility standards legitimately based on the housing program's mission could ensure that
the primary beneficiaries of housing assistance would be inner-
city, poor black households.

First, the creation of a single eligibility/waiting list would ensure
that poor black households would receive at least 60 percent of the
housing assignments (i.e., equal to their proportion of the poor
population metro-wide).

Second, local public housing authorities typically offer vacan-
cies to eligible clients based on length of time on the waiting list.
Though waiting times vary based on household size and housing

mix, the longest waiting periods for housing assignments in the Baltimore region are typically experienced by those on the waiting list for Baltimore City's housing authority. The great bulk of housing assignments in the early years would cut into the waiting list among Baltimore City residents.

Third, it would be a legitimate criterion to assign priority to households that currently reside in the areas of most concentrated poverty. HUD's national policies prevent the construction of new public housing projects in already highly impacted areas. Awarding priority points in the ratings to households living in high-poverty neighborhoods would legitimately focus the opportunity for relocation on those in the most desperate community circumstances.

The organization of a unified, regionwide public housing program will provide the opportunities for relocating inner-city residents to a degree that jurisdiction-by-jurisdiction public housing programs would not.

Through judicious planning and use of the program for residents of existing pockets of suburban poverty, all 11 current poverty neighborhoods in suburban areas could be eliminated and new ones could be prevented from forming. Within Baltimore City, the existing concentrations of poverty will be more resistant. Of 203 census tracts, there are 92 poverty neighborhoods (i.e., 20 percent or more poverty), 35 of which are high- or hyper-poverty neighborhoods (i.e., the poverty level exceeds 40 percent). Reducing the poverty level would require not only helping poor households move out, but also helping to anchor current middle class residents in such neighborhoods and encouraging the movement of other middle class households into the area. However, we can anticipate that the number of poverty neighborhoods would be halved and almost all could be brought below the 40 percent level.

The number of extreme-poverty neighborhoods would be reduced if Baltimore City's Housing Authority aggressively pursued plans to radically revamp their own high-density housing projects. A national model for such an effort comes from an unlikely direction—the notorious Chicago Housing Authority, which in decades past practically *invented* the high-rise, public housing ghetto. Under Chairman Vince Lane's leadership, CHA has received a $50 million grant from HUD to transform the 7,000-resident Cabrini-Green complex, one of the country's most ill-famed projects.

As reported in the *Chicago Tribune* (December 7, 1993), Lane's goal is nothing less than transforming Cabrini-Green into a "normal, mixed income neighborhood." CHA will demolish six high-rise buildings, resulting in the loss of 690 units. Replacing them will be 335 units of low-density housing units in and around Cabrini-Green and another 355 scattered throughout Chicago and its suburbs. Furthermore, Lane wants to resettle as many other Cabrini-Green residents as possible in other CHA-owned scattered site units throughout the city and into privately owned city and suburban rental housing through federal Section 8 rent vouchers.

The second prong of Lane's strategy is to attract working class people into the Cabrini-Green area. Lane is working with developers and local nonprofit housing groups to build new private developments on Cabrini-Green's 70 acres. Three-fourths of the new units will be sold or rented to working class or middle class families. One-quarter will be subsidized by CHA for public housing residents. Lane believes that working class people will be willing to move to the new developments because of the attractiveness of the rapidly regentrifying Near North Side neighborhood and because of the relatively low rents and prices due to CHA subsidies.

The *Tribune* article concludes

> what [Lane and Mayor Richard Daley] are addressing is the economic segregation of the city—the separation of the poor from everyone else. And what their proposals recognize is the harm that such economic segregation has wrought in Chicago, of which the horrendously high rate of crime is just one example. What they want to accomplish is the stabilization of neighborhoods and the city itself. They have a long way to go.

The bottom line is that such results can be achieved in Baltimore—and even in Chicago—through good policy, steady enforcement, and sustained effort. The Baltimore region does not have to achieve miracles. The Baltimore region simply has to work like neighboring Montgomery County.

C. Cost of Purchasing Scattered Site Public Housing

What would this MPDU-type housing program cost? As a housing *construction* policy, a MPDU-type policy would cost nothing—not even to the private developers building under the policy. To compensate developers for selling or renting 15 percent of their units at below-market levels, Metro policies would provide developers with a density bonus. Following the standards developed by Montgomery County, the density bonus would allow developers to build up to 22 percent more units on their sites than would normally be permissible under conventional zoning. Having additional units to sell, based on "free" land, allows developers to recoup profits lost from below-market sales or rentals. With quality design, the higher densities do not detract from the housing developments' aesthetic and environmental qualities. Indeed, promoting more efficient use of undeveloped land should assist in meeting the region's environmental and growth management goals.

As a housing *purchase* policy, however, the cost of the program is significant. We can assume that, on the average, new homes will be priced at an area's median housing value. Table 3.17 shows that in 1990, the median home value for the Baltimore region was $124,000. Under a MPDU-type policy, the price of a home purchased by a moderate-income family would be almost $100,000. The Housing Opportunities Commission would also purchase its 5 percent share of scattered site units at the same price. By buying 500 such units per year, the HOC would have to spend about $50 million per year (at 1990 prices).

It will surely strike many as an outrageous amount of money—$100,000 per unit—to spend on relocating into new homes poor people who don't "deserve" such housing, which may indeed be beyond the financial reach of many hard-working, blue collar families that don't get such a "break."

Such criticisms were constantly leveled against the country's public housing programs in their early decades when design quality, construction standards, and amenities provided in public housing were often superior to what the private market was building. The constant pressure to reduce costs and reduce such perceived inequities eventually resulted in typical public housing projects that "look like public housing."

TABLE 3.17
The annual purchase cost of Metro-HOC's 500
scattered units would be about $50 million

City or County	Median Home Value, 1990	Median HOC Price @ 80%	Units HOC Buys Per Year	Total Annual Cost (millions)
Metro Baltimore	**$124,000**	**$99,182**	**500**	**$49.6**
Baltimore City	$54,700	$60,000	30	$1.8
Anne Arundel County	$127,900	$102,320	110	$11.3
Baltimore County	$99,900	$79,920	125	$10.0
Carroll County	$126,700	$101,360	40	$4.1
Harford County	$114,700	$91,760	70	$6.4
Howard County	$166,500	$133,200	110	$14.7
Queen Anne's County	$118,000	$94,400	15	$1.4

The key to successful mixed-income housing developments is that the units with deep-subsidy tenants must look like all the neighboring units. Montgomery County housing officials often challenge visiting officials to identify which homes or townhouse units in an MPDU project are occupied by "market rate" homeowners, which by subsidized moderate-income families, and which by deep-subsidy tenants. To achieve such seamless integration of poor households into middle class neighborhoods, the program must start with compatible quality in housing structures. High community standards, advice and monitoring from housing counselors, quick and efficient response by the HOC to maintenance needs, and a family's natural pride in responding to opportunity should combine to keep housekeeping standards at middle class neighborhood levels.

In addition, the "affordable" dimension of the housing policies are specifically designed to assist hard-working, moderate-income households achieve just such housing opportunities themselves. Montgomery County's Housing Opportunities Commission, as noted, is also the county's housing finance agency and has extensive low-interest, low-down-payment loan programs to help moderate-income households step up into home ownership.

The most common objection that is openly voiced by middle class homeowners to the presence of moderate- and low-income housing is that it will drive down the price or appreciation of their own property. Of course, under Montgomery County's MPDU policy, the *housing* quality is the same (or, at least, at a high standard). The anxiety arises, then, on the basis of the impact on housing values of having low- and moderate-income *neighbors*.

The Montgomery County government commissioned an independent study of the relative appreciation of home values in 1988. An area builder, William L. Berry & Company, Ltd., analyzed resale records for single-family homes and townhouses in 20 comparable projects throughout the county. Ten had MPDU properties; ten did not. The study found that the MPDU communities averaged an annual 14.28 percent increase in resale value, while the non-MPDU communities averaged only a 10.30 percent annual appreciation.

The big news, of course, is that resale values in MPDU communities in Montgomery County neither went down nor increased at a slower rate than non-MPDU communities. In addition, county officials note that there have been no noticeable social problems in MPDU communities. In this context, in addressing why MPDU resale values rose faster than non-MPDU values, the researchers note that the one constant characteristic of all MPDU communities is that these communities must have 50 units or more. Since MPDU communities are medium- to large-sized, they are more likely to offer amenities such as swimming pools, clubhouses, and tennis courts, which may not be offered in communities of fewer than 50 units. This may be one factor that accounts for the higher appreciation rates for MPDU communities.

The study concludes *"clearly this study demonstrates that on average the existence of MPDUs in a community does not slow home appreciation rates as compared to communities without MPDUs* [emphasis *not* added]."

4. Creating a Regional Tax Base Sharing Program

If the Baltimore region needs to embrace neighboring Montgomery County's planning, zoning, and housing policies, the Baltimore region should also emulate farther off metropolitan Minneapolis–St. Paul in implementing a tax base sharing program. The objectives would be

1. to share the tax revenues generated by regional growth more equitably with all jurisdictions;

2. to allow movement toward the equalization of Baltimore City's property tax rate with suburban levels, thereby reducing the competitive disadvantage the central city suffers for retaining or attracting middle class residents and businesses; and

3. to help finance the operations of Metro, in particular, the budget of its Housing Opportunities Commission to purchase additional public housing units under Metro's MPDU-type housing policies.

A. Tax Base Trends[17]

To understand why such a program is necessary and how it might work, we need first to examine the evolution of the property tax base throughout the region. Table 3.18 shows the proportion of all

---

[17]Since Tables 3.18–3.25 are intended to be illustrative rather than definitive, we chose to use data from 1966 to 1986 (i.e., from the quinquennial censuses, beginning in 1967 through 1987) to ensure comparability of data. Though Baltimore City has continued to experience some commercial and industrial tax base revival through its downtown redevelopment efforts, updating the information would not show a reversal of overall trends depicted, particularly in residential values. In addition, the Census of Governments does not provide data for Queen Anne's County for the earliest years. Thus, Queen Anne's County was excluded from the tables; however, it would be covered by the Metro Tax Base Pool.

TABLE 3.18
Proportion of the Baltimore region's commercial/industrial properties
(by value) for local jurisdictions, 1966–1986

City or County	Value Commercial/ Industrial, 1966	Value Commercial/ Industrial, 1971	Value Commercial/ Industrial, 1976	Value Commercial/ Industrial, 1981	Value Commercial/ Industrial, 1986
Metro Baltimore	100%	100%	100%	100%	100%
Baltimore City	55%	47%	37%	29%	31%
Anne Arundel County	7%	10%	13%	16%	17%
Baltimore County	32%	34%	34%	39%	32%
Carroll County	1%	2%	3%	3%	4%
Harford County	2%	3%	4%	5%	4%
Howard County	2%	3%	9%	9%	12%

locally assessed commercial and industrial property by jurisdiction of location from 1966 to 1986. Having contained 55 percent of the value of all commercial and industrial property in the metro area in 1966, Baltimore City's share declined to 31 percent by 1986. (Through the intensive effort at redeveloping Downtown Baltimore and the Inner Harbor, Baltimore City did reverse its decline in the 1980s, edging back upward from 29 percent in 1981 to 31 percent of the commercial/industrial tax base.) By 1986, Baltimore County (32 percent) had edged past the city as the largest location of commercial and industrial property; but in the late 1980s, even Baltimore County was slowly losing position to the booming outer counties.

For residential property value, however, Table 3.19 shows that Baltimore City's decline has been continuous. Containing 38 percent of the value of all of the metro area's residential property in 1966, Baltimore City dropped precipitously in the next decade to 21 percent. Thereafter, it declined more slowly but steadily to an 18 percent share by 1986. By the end of the 1980s, though Baltimore County had twice the residential property value of Baltimore City, Baltimore County's proportion had stabilized around 36 percent in the face of the more vigorous residential growth of Anne Arundel and Howard Counties.

B. Tax Base Sharing Plan

The proposed tax base sharing program is modeled on the Twin Cities' Fiscal Disparities Program. Like the Twin Cities model, the proposed Maryland state law would require that all local jurisdic-

TABLE 3.19
Proportion of residential property (by value) for local jurisdictions,
1966–1986

City or County	Value Residential Property, 1966	Value Residential Property, 1971	Value Residential Property, 1976	Value Residential Property, 1981	Value Residential Property, 1986
Metro Baltimore	100%	100%	100%	100%	100%
Baltimore City	38%	30%	21%	19%	18%
Anne Arundel County	14%	17%	19%	22%	23%
Baltimore County	37%	39%	40%	36%	36%
Carroll County	3%	4%	4%	5%	5%
Harford County	5%	6%	8%	7%	7%
Howard County	3%	3%	8%	10%	11%

tions in the metro area allocate 40 percent of the incremental growth in commercial and industrial property valuation to a regional tax base pool. In addition, the Maryland law would require allocating to the common pool 40 percent of the incremental growth in residential property tax for residences valued above 150 percent of the regional median housing value.

Targeting only higher-end housing would have several positive effects. First, it would discourage local communities from engaging systematically in "fiscal zoning"—the practice of setting lot requirements, density levels, and the like to allow for only high-end housing. Second, it would encourage more efficient use of available land, particularly that already served by existing utilities and other public infrastructure. Third, it would reward local communities for encouraging more moderate-priced housing, since the communities would keep 100 percent of the property tax revenues generated from lesser-priced housing for local use.

Local jurisdictions would continue to set their own property tax rates for (1) all of their current property valuation as of the base year and (2) all of the property contained in their 60 percent share of incremental growth. However, the Metro Council would set uniform commercial/industrial tax rates throughout the region for all property in the common tax base pool.

C. Allocating the Commercial/ Industrial Tax Base Pool

How would the tax base system work, and what would its impact be? Let us illustrate the system by taking a look at the size and location of growth in the property tax base in past decades. What would the impact have been if this policy had been in effect for a recent 20-year period? Table 3.20 shows the growth in the region's commercial/industrial (C/I) tax base between 1966 and 1986. Regionwide, the commercial/industrial tax base grew from $1.2 billion in 1966 to $4.8 billion in 1986. (Some of the increase was the result of the inflation of values as opposed to new construction and equipment installation.) Of the $3.6 billion increase by 1986 (in the 1986 allocation formula), 60 percent, or $2.2 billion, would remain with the local jurisdiction in which it was located, and 40 percent, or $1.4 billion, would be allocated to the regional tax base pool.

Table 3.21 illustrates the methodology by which the reallocation factor for each jurisdiction is developed. Column E lists the total property tax base per capita for each jurisdiction in 1986. Column F shows each jurisdiction's percentage increase or decrease over the metro area's average tax base per capita. (The metro average is $10,369 in taxable property per capita.) Column G lists each jurisdiction's share of the metro area's population in 1986. Finally, Column H divides each jurisdiction's population percentage by its index of tax base per capita to produce that jurisdiction's allocation factor. Thus, for 1986, Baltimore City's allocated share of the pooled commercial/industrial tax base is 49 percent, Anne Arundel County's share is 13 percent, and so on.

The final steps are summarized in Table 3.22. For 1986, each jurisdiction's share of the reallocated tax base pool is listed in Column I. Column I is calculated by multiplying the total C/I tax base in the pool ($1,435,993,000) by each jurisdiction's allocation factor (Column H in Table 3.21). Column J shows the net change from what each jurisdiction initially contributed (Column D in Table 3.20) to what each jurisdiction was allocated in return (Column I). Thus, in 1986, Baltimore City could have benefited from

TABLE 3.20
Regional growth in the commercial/industrial tax base, 1966–1986
(in millions of dollars)

City or County	A C/I Tax Base, 1966	B C/I Tax Base, 1986	C 60% C/I Gain, 1986	D 40% C/I Gain, 1986
Metro Baltimore	**$1,242**	**$4,832**	**$2,154**	**$1,436**
Baltimore City	$686	$1,487	$481	$320
Anne Arundel County	$84	$827	$446	$297
Baltimore County	$400	$1,559	$695	$464
Carroll County	$17	$179	$97	$65
Harford County	$30	$208	$107	$71
Howard County	$25	$572	$328	$219

Camden Yards Is Only the Latest Chapter in the Running Story of "Baltimore's Stadium." Its Predecessor, Memorial Stadium, Was a Gussied Up "Municipal Stadium"—Built in 1922!

Opening Day at Oriole Park at Camden Yards Stadium was April 6, 1992, and the team and the town had to go some to better the show Baltimore mounted for the "new" Memorial Stadium in 1954.

That "new" needs some explaining. In 1954 the team wasn't new. The old St. Louis Browns became the Baltimore Orioles, but the stadium was a $6 million redo of what was once, tracing its beginnings to 1922, Municipal Stadium. The Baltimore Orioles of the International League played there following the 1944 fire that burned down their home, Oriole Park at Greenmount and 29th. Municipal/Memorial Stadium was gussied up in a major-league way for Baltimore's major-league team.

To the Spartan, horseshoe-shaped Municipal Stadium, which had been designed for football (Navy played Notre Dame there), were added the upper deck, 20,000 plus additional seats, many chair-back seats to take the place of traditional wooden benches, the mezzanine, a new administration building, light towers and new facade on 33rd St. George Weiss, then vice president of the powerhouse Yankee organiza-

tion who visited the place a week before opening day, said, "I'm surprised with its vastness, and I'm pleased with its overall design for playing and watching. I just hope it'll be ready for opening day."

Weiss had reason to fear; it took a lot of hustle and hurry-up (and overtime) to get the job done.

In the opener, the Orioles beat the White Sox 3–1 before 46,354 delirious fans. Clint Courtney and Vern Stephens hit homers; Bob Turley pitched a seven-hitter. Vice President Richard Nixon threw out the first ball.

But the feeling of newness—of the team and the stadium—was best expressed in an outpouring of noise, confetti, floats, balloons, music, and love that characterized the celebration parade.

It began at 34th and Charles near Johns Hopkins. Brass bands, beauty queens, merchants' floats, elected officials (though Mayor Thomas D'Alesandro had to watch on television from his room at Bon Secours Hospital), civic organizations, servicemen and women in dress uniforms, clowns, and of course, the uni-

Continued on page 128

TABLE 3.21
Methodology and source of information needed to determine
allocation factor for commercial/industrial tax pool

City or County	E Total Tax Base per Capita, 1986	F Index Metro Tax Base per Capita	G % Share Metro Population	H Alloca- tion Factor, 1986
Metro Baltimore	**$10,369**	**100%**	**100%**	**100%**
Baltimore City	$6,333	61%	33%	49%
Anne Arundel County	$12,621	122%	18%	13%
Baltimore County	$11,985	116%	30%	23%
Carroll County	$10,816	104%	5%	5%
Harford County	$9,946	96%	7%	6%
Howard County	$17,359	167%	7%	4%

receiving an increase of $384 million in its C/I tax base, while
Anne Arundel County's C/I tax base would have been reduced by
$110 million.

However, as Table 3.22 further demonstrates, such net gains
and losses leave intact the great bulk of a jurisdiction's tax base.
Anne Arundel County's total C/I tax base would have been $717
million, composed of its pre-1966 C/I value ($84 million from
Table 3.20, Column A), its retention of 60 percent of the subse-
quent growth ($446 million from Table 3.20, Column C), and its
reallocation from the C/I pool ($187 from Table 3.22, Column I).
Thus, despite having been one of the region's most vigorous

TABLE 3.22
Baltimore City gains 31% additional C/I tax base
through the Metro tax pool plan

City or County	I C/I Base Alloca- tion, 1986	J C/I Base Net Change, 1986	K Total C/I Tax Base, 1986	L % Original C/I Base
Metro Baltimore	**$1,436**	**$0**	**$4,832**	**100%**
Baltimore City	$704	$384	$1,871	126%
Anne Arundel County	$187	−$110	$717	87%
Baltimore County	$330	−$134	$1,425	91%
Carroll County	$72	$7	$186	104%
Harford County	$86	$15	$223	107%
Howard County	$57	−$162	$410	72%

CAMDEN YARDS IS ONLY THE LATEST CHAPTER IN THE RUNNING STORY OF "BALTIMORE'S STADIUM."
(continued)

formed ballplayers themselves headed down Charles St. They threw plastic baseballs to the crowd, estimated at 350,000.

"It's the culmination of great dream," said Clarence Miles, who, with Mayor D'Alesandro helped bring the team to Baltimore.

A lot of people who were there surely relive still the color and music and civic good will that came together that day.

And remember, too, the circuitous route the city had to take to get there!

---

growth centers, it would have retained 87 percent of its jurisdictional C/I tax base (Column L, Table 3.22).

By contrast, Baltimore City would have increased its effective C/I tax base by 26 percent above the value of C/I properties actually located in the city. Carroll County and Harford County would also have registered modest gains for 1986, while Baltimore County (91 percent) and Howard County (72 percent) would have joined Anne Arundel County as net contributors.

D. Allocating the Residential Tax Base Pool

The next tables—Tables 3.23 and Table 3.24—repeat the same steps for residential tax base in 1986. (The table calculating the allocation factor is omitted, since the same factor applies to both residential and C/I property.) The proposed policy affecting residential property would be to pool 40 percent of the value of only residential property at 150 percent of the metropolitan median value. As a shortcut in characterizing how much of residential tax base would be based on structures 150 percent above the median, the assumption is made that only half of the increase was attributable to the higher-value residential properties. Thus, the mathematical outcome of that assumption is equivalent to having local jurisdictions retain 80 percent (not 60 percent) of the increment in residential value and contribute only 20 percent to the regional pool.

TABLE 3.23
Regional growth in residential tax base between 1966 and 1986
(in millions of dollars)

City or County	M Residential Tax Base, 1966	N Residential Tax Base, 1986	O 80% Residential Gain, 1986	P 20% Residential Gain, 1986
Metro Baltimore	$3,536	$17,293	$11,007	$2,752
Baltimore City	$1,360	$3,180	$1,456	$364
Anne Arundel County	$500	$4,051	$2,841	$710
Baltimore County	$1,294	$6,146	$3,881	$970
Carroll County	$99	$843	$595	$149
Harford County	$161	$1,222	$849	$212
Howard County	$122	$1,851	$1,384	$346

Since residential property regionwide accounts for over two-thirds of the total tax base, the dollar values affected are much larger. In 1986, the residential tax base pooled ($2.7 billion) would be almost twice the C/I tax base pooled ($1.4 billion). At the end of the process, Baltimore City would be the beneficiary of an additional $1.0 billion in reallocated tax base, an increase of 31 percent above the value of residential property actually located in the city. All suburban jurisdictions would be net contributors, ranging from Harford County (–1 percent) to Howard County (–13 percent).

If we look at the combined impact of both the commercial/industrial and residential tax base pools (Table 3.25), for our sam-

TABLE 3.24
Baltimore City gains 36% more residential tax base
through Metro Tax Base Pool

City or County	Q Residential Base Allocation, 1986	R Residential Base Net Change, 1986	S Total Residential Tax Base, 1986	T % Original Residential Base
Metro Baltimore	$2,752	$0	$17,293	100%
Baltimore City	$1,348	$984	$4,164	131%
Anne Arundel County	$358	–$352	$3,699	91%
Baltimore County	$633	–$337	$5,808	95%
Carroll County	$138	–$11	$832	99%
Harford County	$165	–$47	$1,175	96%
Howard County	$110	–$236	$1,616	87%

TABLE 3.25
Baltimore City and Harford County are net recipients
under the combined Metro Tax Base Pool for 1986

City or County	U C/I Base Net Change, 1986	V Residential Base Net Change, 1986	W Total Tax Base Change	X Total Revised Tax Base, 1986	Y % of Original Total Base
Metro Baltimore	$0	$0	$0	$22,125	100%
Baltimore City	$384	$984	$1,368	$6,035	129%
Anne Arundel County	–$110	–$352	–$462	$4,416	91%
Baltimore County	–$134	–$337	–$471	$7,233	94%
Carroll County	$7	–$11	–$4	$1,018	100%
Harford County	$15	–$47	$32	$1,398	98%
Howard County	–$162	–$236	–$398	$2,026	84%

ple year 1986, there is only one net beneficiary. Baltimore City would have had a 29 percent gain over its jurisdictional base. Harford County's gains in C/I tax base would have almost offset losses in the residential tax base. Anne Arundel and Howard Counties, the two most vigorously growing areas during this period, would have been the largest net contributors, experiencing net reductions of 9 percent and 16 percent, respectively, in their overall tax base.

E. Setting the Property Tax Rate

All of the calculations in the preceding sections dealt with pooling a share of the local jurisdictions' property *tax base* under Metro's administration. This section will address the property *tax rate* to be applied to that common pool, the estimated property *taxes generated*, and how the funds would be used (if not automatically rebated to the covered jurisdictions).

Property tax rates are sharply different between Baltimore City and its suburban counties, as shown in Table 3.26. Baltimore City's much higher rate (5.95 percent) is not primarily the result of rapacious city politicians and mismanaged municipal government, as some critics of America's big cities would have one believe. The higher rates are primarily the result of the factors discussed in previous chapters: the inelastic city's inability to expand to capture new, low-density growth; the shrinking tax base (at least in relative terms); the extraordinary costs of housing a disproportionate number of poor people in the city; and the constant struggle to make ends meet. Meanwhile, all such factors

TABLE 3.26
Local property tax rates in 1990

City or County	Property Tax Rate, 1990
Baltimore Region	**N/A**
Baltimore City	5.95%
Anne Arundel County	2.51%
Baltimore County	2.90%
Carroll County	2.35%
Harford County	2.73%
Howard County	2.49%

work in reverse to the advantage of Baltimore City's suburbs. It is true that there are many well-managed suburban governments. It is also true that it is easy to be well managed—and have low tax rates (2.35 percent to 2.90 percent)—when a suburban community has few people with special needs and a constantly expanding tax base.

Baltimore area businesses and homeowners are not being taxed at these rates (i.e., 2.35–5.95 percent) based on the full market value of their properties. The Maryland Department of Taxation and Revenue sets annually an "assessment ratio" that averages about 40 percent of fair market value per jurisdiction. (All of the property values presented in Tables 3.18–3.23 reflect this state-reduced valuation.)

As was recommended above, under the tax base pool, the Metro Council would have the authority and responsibility to set uniform tax rates for commercial/industrial and residential property covered in the pool. For illustration's sake, assume that the Metro Council sets the pooled tax rate at 4.00 percent per $100 of assessed valuation for all pooled property. Table 3.27 demonstrates what the resulting tax rate would be for new commercial/industrial construction and residential construction (i.e., for homes not exceeding 150 percent of the area's median value) in the different jurisdictions.

These would represent *maximum* tax rates applicable to new construction. Any tax rate increase in suburban areas (or tax rate decrease within Baltimore City) would be very small and slow, reflecting the rate of appreciation of property values for existing property. For example, if a high-end home in Baltimore County appreciated 5 percent in assessed value, only 40 percent of that 5 percent increment in value would be captured by the metro pool and assessed at the pool rate of 4.00 percent rather than Baltimore

FINALLY DEDICATED IN 1983, THE BALTIMORE CIVIC CENTER TRACES ITS ORIGINS 37 YEARS EARLIER TO THE INTERESTS OF AIRCRAFT TYCOON, GLENN L. MARTIN! Plans Called for It to be Built in Druid Hill Park— the Park Board Shouted, "Rape!"

Just after World War II, aircraft tycoon Glenn L. Martin, responding to citizen interest in a Baltimore civic center, proposed a stadium with an air-supported roof. He was called "a crazy dreamer," and all that happened was that the city improved Municipal Stadium.

The Chamber of Commerce (later the Greater Baltimore Committee) joined the quest, calling for private financing of a center. That hope died aborning, and the committee laid the financing problem on Mayor Thomas D'Alesandro, Jr. He promptly tossed it to the state, which got a $6,000,000 civic center loan on the ballot. The voters, in a careless mood they were to regret, approved it without even knowing where the center was to be built. That inattention to details was to create one of the stormiest chapters in the political history of the city.

Studies at the time suggested more than 30 locations, including Mount Royal Station, Pimlico Race Track, Fort Carroll, City Hospitals, Druid Hill Park, Carlin's Park at Park Circle, Lake Clifton—and over (on stilts, as it were) what is now the Jones Falls Expressway.

The Chamber, after "careful study of all the facts," came in with its "final recommendation"—Carlin's Park, at the convergence of Park Heights and Reisterstown Road. Downtown interests raised a ruckus, claiming that putting the center "all the way out in the country" will take business away from downtown. They suggested Sam Smith Park (now Harborplace).

In one of the hottest Augusts on record, 1957, in one of the most bizarre acts in the history of Baltimore's bizarre politics, Mayor D'Alesandro dropped a bombshell: He announced that he had decided that the Civic Center would be built on the edge of Druid Hill Lake. The citizenry screamed; Samuel ("Sam") Hammerman, president of the Park Board, called a special session of the City Council to deal with the crisis; Comptroller Hyman Pressman took the city to court, and ultimately the council's approval of the mayor's proposal was ruled illegal.

An exhausted electorate and a mayor out of patience finally agreed (June 4, 1958) on Hopkins Place, a location that wasn't one of the sites originally pro-
Continued on page 134

TABLE 3.27
Proposed new tax rates for growth in jurisdictions

City or County	Current Tax Rate, 1990	Pool Tax Rate, 1990	Combined Tax Rate, 1990	% of City Rate Before	% of City Rate After
Baltimore Region	N/A	N/A	N/A	N/A	N/A
Baltimore City	5.95%	4.00%	5.17%	100%	100%
Anne Arundel County	2.51%	4.00%	3.11%	42%	60%
Baltimore County	2.90%	4.00%	3.34%	49%	65%
Carroll County	2.35%	4.00%	3.01%	39%	58%
Harford County	2.73%	4.00%	3.24%	46%	63%
Howard County	2.49%	4.00%	3.09%	42%	60%

County's 2.90 percent rate. The combined tax rate on the home-owner's tax bill would be 2.92 percent.

How much property tax revenue would our illustrative rate yield from the pool? If we used our illustration of the size of the pool in 1986 (as if the policy had been in effect for 20 years), the total amount of pooled tax base would be $4.2 billion (i.e., $1.436 billion in C/I tax base and $2.752 billion in residential tax base). Table 3.28 shows the amount of taxes that businesses and home-owners would pay for new or appreciated properties before and after the plan's implementation.

Furthermore, as demonstrated in Table 3.29, the net changes are not very large when compared with each jurisdiction's total property tax collections for the demonstration year.

TABLE 3.28
Twenty-year total in base, pool, and net taxes paid by
jurisdictions under the Metro plan
(in millions of dollars)

City or County	Tax Base Pool, Demo. Year	Before Plan Taxes Paid, Demo. Year	After Plan Taxes, Demo. Year	Net Taxes Paid With Plan, Demo. Year
Baltimore Region	$4,188	$134	$168	$33
Baltimore City	$684	$41	$27	–$14
Anne Arundel County	$1,007	$25	$40	$15
Baltimore County	$1,434	$42	$57	$16
Carroll County	$214	$5	$9	$4
Harford County	$283	$8	$11	$3
Howard County	$565	$14	$23	$9

Finally Dedicated in 1983, the Baltimore Civic Center Traces Its Origins 37 Years Earlier to the Interests of Aircraft Tycoon, Glenn L. Martin!
(continued)

posed. The Civic Center was dedicated March 30, 1963.

Mayor J. Harold Grady presided over the dedication. Former Mayor Tommy D'Alesandro did not attend.

F. Using the Funds—Housing First

All of the above illustrations are based on what the program might look like in its twentieth year (using 1966 to 1986 as the study period and 1986 as the demonstration year). In reality, the tax base sharing program will start small, since it operates only on incremental growth. Moving forward in time from the demonstration year, what would be a realistic outlook of the potential of the tax base sharing program?

Total assessed value in the Baltimore metro area was about $42 billion in 1993. About 94 percent of that total, or $40 billion, was in commercial, industrial, and residential property. New construction and appreciation of existing property values (through inflation) average about 5 percent annually. Thus, for 1994, the increment of growth would be about $2 billion.

One-fifth of this would be attributed to commercial/industrial growth, or $400 million. Applying the metro pool's share of 40 percent of the incremental growth would yield a pooled commercial/industrial tax base of $160 million. A tax rate of 4 percent would yield $6.4 million in new taxes from the C/I tax base pool.

Turning to the residential side, four-fifths, or $1.6 billion, of the growth would be from residential property. If we assume that only half of this would be from properties in excess of 150 percent of the median home value and then apply the pool's 40 percent share, the pool's residential tax base would be $320 million. A tax rate of 4 percent would yield $12.8 million in new taxes from the residential tax base pool.

TABLE 3.29
A 4 percent tax pool rate increases property taxes in region by
$33 million, or less than 5 percent of the current level
(in millions of dollars)

City or County	Total Tax Base, Demo. Year	Actual Taxes Paid, Demo. Year	Net New Taxes Paid, Demo. Year	Net % Change, Demo. Year
Baltimore Region	**$22,125**	**$747**	**$33**	**4.4%**
Baltimore City	$4,667	$278	–$14	–4.8%
Anne Arundel County	$4,878	$122	$15	12.3%
Baltimore County	$7,705	$223	$16	7.1%
Carroll County	$1,022	$24	$4	14.7%
Harford County	$1,430	$39	$3	9.2%
Howard County	$2,423	$60	$9	14.1%

Thus, in a hypothetical first year of the program (1994), the total revenue generated for the metro pool would be $19.2 million from one year's incremental growth, while local governments would collect about $53 million in new revenues from incremental growth. This $53 million in revenues from incremental growth in property values would be added to the almost $1.5 billion in property taxes already collected from the prior tax base that was exempted from the regional tax base pool.

Given the modest fiscal weight of the regional pool in its initial years, the Metro Council should *not* reallocate any of the funds back to local governments for general governmental purposes. Instead, the Metro Council should appropriate the maximum amount possible to its own Housing Opportunities Commission for acquisition of scattered site public housing under its metrowide MPDU-type policy. With an annual target of 500 new units available per year, this first-year yield of $19 million would permit acquisition of about 190 units. It is hoped that with judicious use of federal grants-in-aid for housing assistance, the program could purchase 300–350 units in its first year.

Table 3.30, however, demonstrates how steadily the metro tax base pool and actual taxes in the Metro fund build up. Assuming 5 percent growth in assessed valuation metro-wide, the Metro fund rises from $19 million in the first year to $39 million in the second year to $60 million by the third year. At that point, the Metro Council can choose among alternative strategies, such as (1) allocating additional funds to the Housing Opportunities Commission

Table 3.30
Current year and cumulative tax base and tax pool for
20 years under proposed tax basing sharing plan
(in billions of dollars)

Year of Metro Tax Pool	Current Year's Tax Base	Next Year's Tax Base	Current Pool Tax Base	Cumulative Pool Tax Base	Current Year Tax Increase	Annual Tax Pool
1	$40.00	$42.00	$0.48	$0.48	$0.019	$0.019
2	$42.00	$44.10	$0.50	$0.98	$0.020	$0.039
3	$44.10	$46.31	$0.52	$1.50	$0.021	$0.060
4	$46.31	$48.62	$0.55	$2.05	$0.022	$0.082
5	$48.62	$51.05	$0.58	$2.63	$0.023	$0.105
6	$51.05	$53.60	$0.61	$3.24	$0.024	$0.129
7	$53.60	$56.28	$0.64	$3.87	$0.025	$0.155
8	$56.28	$59.10	$0.67	$4.54	$0.027	$0.181
9	$59.10	$62.05	$0.70	$5.24	$0.028	$0.210
10	$62.05	$65.16	$0.74	$5.98	$0.029	$0.239
11	$65.16	$68.41	$0.77	$6.75	$0.031	$0.270
12	$68.41	$71.83	$0.81	$7.57	$0.032	$0.302
13	$71.83	$75.43	$0.85	$8.42	$0.034	$0.337
14	$75.43	$79.20	$0.90	$9.31	$0.036	$0.372
15	$79.20	$83.16	$0.94	$10.25	$0.038	$0.410
16	$83.16	$87.31	$0.99	$11.24	$0.039	$0.449
17	$87.31	$91.68	$1.04	$12.28	$0.041	$0.491
18	$91.68	$96.26	$1.09	$13.37	$0.044	$0.535
19	$96.26	$101.08	$1.14	$14.51	$0.046	$0.580
20	$101.08	$106.13	$1.20	$15.71	$0.048	$0.628

either to purchase existing units in existing neighborhoods or expand the rent voucher program or (2) beginning to allocate tax receipts back to local jurisdictions.

With regard to distribution of funds back to local governments, initial distributions should be limited to Baltimore City, which already exceeds its fair share of poverty. The Metro Council should adopt a sliding scale in which tax reallocations are triggered by different milestones reached by suburban jurisdictions in terms of their fair share targets. One incentive method might be for the Housing Opportunities Commission to make payments in lieu of taxes ("PILOT") to local governments equal to what would be paid if HOC-owned units had remained in private ownership. Thus, sharing in the Metro Tax Base Pool would be structurally linked to sharing in the regional housing program for low-income households.

By the twentieth year of the program, as illustrated in Table 3.30, the Metro Tax Base Pool would have risen to $15.7 billion, about 15 percent of the metro area's entire tax base ($106 billion). The pool would be generating $628 million of revenues in its twentieth year—sufficient to meet all Metro's housing policy requirements and provide for major reallocations back to local governments for general governmental purposes.

But more important, the region would have substantially met its target of allowing for the voluntary and more equitable settlement of poor black and poor white households throughout the region. Harford, Howard, and Queen Anne's Counties would have met their goals by utilizing only 5 percent of new housing constructed in larger developments (i.e., 50 or more units). There could be minimal use of existing housing in existing neighborhoods in those counties. Carroll, Anne Arundel, and Baltimore Counties would have met at least 60 percent of their goals through these policies affecting new construction. Purchasing existing housing and using rent vouchers judiciously in existing apartment complexes would accomplish the balance.

All could have been achieved without financial reliance on additional housing subsidies from the federal and state governments. It could be self-financed through tapping the region's natural growth without taking away any *current* revenues from local governments.

In the previous two sections, I tried to illustrate how the metro-wide fair share housing proposals and a tax base sharing pool would work. The key word is *illustrate*. Both draw on past trends to try to project future realities. The data need updating. Where new housing was built from 1970 to 1990 is clearly not exactly where new housing will be built in the next 20 years. What the discussion of past housing patterns most illustrates is what Baltimore City and its suburbs might be like today if these housing recommendations had been put in place more than 20 years ago.

In similar fashion, the property tax base data is out of date. It covers the period from 1966 to 1986. The data used does have the virtue of consistency and uniformity. All comes from a single source, the *Census of Governments*, conducted every five years by the U.S. Census Bureau. The data could have been updated from state and local records, but would the definitions and methodology used to calculate property tax base in the 1990s be consistent with the way in which tax base data was reported for the 1960s? I couldn't be sure, so I opted for consistency rather than being up to date.[18]

What I've tried to illustrate in these sections, however, are some simple truths.

First, the problem is not the scope but the concentration of urban poverty. Of every hundred residents of metro Baltimore (the real "city"), only four are poor and white, and only six are poor and black. Poor whites are substantially integrated into the larger metro community; 60 percent of poor whites live in the suburbs, and three out of four live in middle class neighborhoods. By contrast, 86 percent of poor blacks live in Baltimore City, and three out of four poor blacks live in poverty neighborhoods.

Second, with a commitment to become an open society, more integrated by race and income, substantial progress can be made. Over a 20-year period, a regionwide fair share housing program, targeting primarily new construction, can cut the *concentration* of poverty in half in Baltimore City—and will probably reduce the overall poverty level in the region as well.

Third, the Baltimore area can afford to carry out this program in economic terms. Acquiring the necessary scattered site housing would cost $50 million a year. That's a lot of money. At the same time, that is barely one-tenth of 1 percent of the $40 billion income reported by Baltimore area residents in the 1990 census.

The point is simple. If a community does the right thing— which it can afford to do—over a sustained period of time, it will solve the problem.

---

[18]As this book was in final preparation, the *1992 Census of Governments* published its first survey of 1991 property valuation by state and county (but without any breakdown by category). It shows a slight decline of both Baltimore City and Baltimore County's share of regional property valuation.

	1986	1991
Baltimore City	21%	20%
Anne Arundel County	22%	23%
Baltimore County	34%	33%
Carroll County	5%	5%
Harford County	7%	7%
Howard County	11%	12%

CONCLUSION

On December 20, 1994, the federal government designated the poorest area of the City of Baltimore an "empowerment zone." Designation brought $100 million in hard cash and special tax breaks estimated to be worth $225 million if all job creation hopes are met over a ten-year period. The program's planners estimated that another $800 million in city, state, and private funds (mostly mortgage commitments) would be triggered by the federal funds.

City and neighborhood leaders greeted the action joyfully. Said one neighborhood leader, "We are the recipients of God's Christmas present."

Actually, it was the Clinton Administration's Christmas present to Baltimore City and five other cities (Atlanta, Chicago, Detroit, New York, and Philadelphia-Camden). In keeping with the federal government's customary generosity in any season, six other cities became "supplemental empowerment zones" or "enhanced enterprise communities" (Los Angeles, Cleveland, Boston, Oakland, Houston, and Kansas City), receiving $25–125 million grants but no tax incentives, and 60 other urban communities were designated "enterprise communities," receiving $3 million grants.

Baltimore City's 6.8-square-mile empowerment zone brackets downtown, targeting many of the city's poorest neighborhoods. The West Baltimore section includes Sandtown-Winchester and Pigtown. The East Baltimore section takes in the neighborhoods around the Johns Hopkins medical institutions. The Fairfield section of South Baltimore is ticketed for industrial development. In all, the zone has over 72,000 residents, 41 percent of whom are poor. With about 10 percent of the city's population, the areas account for 21 percent of the city's murders and 23 percent of the drug arrests.

The one-time grant of $100 million in hard cash from the federal government will pay for a wide variety of health, job training, and economic development programs over the next five years.

- $32.4 million in education and job training programs, including a six-week, $400 per week training fund for on-the-job experience and a nonprofit van pool to transport workers to jobs that are not accessible by public transportation;
- $25.8 million to set up neighborhood Family Resource Centers and Child Development Resource Centers;
- $21.3 million for economic development, including an "ecological-industrial park" in Fairfield and a One-Stop Capital Shop to provide $20 million in revolving credit for businesses located in the zone;
- $6.9 million for "community mobilization," largely by supporting eight "Village Center" offices;
- $4.2 million for housing, primarily as seed money to stimulate establishment of a $20 million mortgage pool to help zone residents buy or renovate homes (with a goal of raising home ownership from 30 percent to 50 percent);
- $900,000 as seed money to establish a $15 million community development bank to pay for housing rehabilitation, commercial revitalization, and entrepreneurial development in the East Baltimore section;
- $3.4 million for public safety to deploy "mobile police stations" in high-crime areas and open-air drug markets and to provide incentives for police officers to live in the zone; and
- $5 million for administration, evaluation, and monitoring.

The *Baltimore Sun* reported that "a key component of the empowerment zone is job creation, with businesses qualifying for tax credits for each zone resident trained and hired. Within two years, officials estimate, 557 jobs will be created at an annual salary of $14,560. After 10 years, they say, there will be 8,885 new jobs for zone residents at an annual salary of $17,056."

"This is probably the single most important influx of federal funds this city has ever gotten," said U.S. Senator Barbara Mikulski, who lobbied HUD hard for the designation. "It will help ensure Baltimore will have a future into the next century."

Two Paths to Baltimore's Future

What kind of a future will the empowerment zone bring Baltimore City? Let me offer two alternative assessments. My expectations are based on 30 years' experience in urban affairs, which began with my involvement in the War on Poverty–sponsored "community action program" in the heart of Washington, D.C.'s poorest neighborhoods in the mid-1960s; continued during my years as the U.S. Manpower Administration's legislative chief, as creator and director of Albuquerque's Comprehensive Manpower Program and someone who was active in Albuquerque's model cities program, as mayor of Albuquerque and local "prime sponsor" of the Labor Department's Comprehensive Employment and Training Act (CETA) and of HUD's annual Community Development Block Grants (CDBG); and includes more recent involvement with the federal Job Training Partnership Act. My hands-on experiences are buttressed by my having analyzed social and economic dynamics for all of America's 320 metro areas and having studied, consulted, and spoken in over 60 metro areas since publication of *Cities without Suburbs* in April 1993.

The Assessments: The Baltimore Area Can Follow One of Two Paths

Path 1: The empowerment zone program can be carried out within the context of the regionwide housing strategies I have advocated. This would result in a substantial proportion of the zone's poor households seizing the opportunity to move out to make new futures in nonpoor, largely suburban neighborhoods. The impact of the empowerment zone program would then help to anchor existing middle class households in the zone and attract others. Few new zone-based enterprises would actually be created. However, several target neighborhoods would become more attractive investment sites for new and renovated housing for professionals employed downtown or at the Johns Hopkins medical complex. With more racially and economically diverse populations, some empowerment zone neighborhoods would make a slow but steady comeback. Crime rates would fall. Neighborhood retail businesses would revive modestly. Independent "charter schools" would provide better educational quality alternatives to local public schools. *In short, the program would be a modest but steady success because it would be a smaller (but important) element of a regionwide strategy for ending the concentration of poverty.* Within a public policy framework of promoting diversity, balance, and stability everywhere, empowerment zone programs would help to diversify, balance, and stabilize the empowerment zone neighborhoods themselves, but they would not be expected to be the primary path to economic opportunity and self-sufficiency for most of the area's poorest current residents.

Path 2: State and local political leaders would seize on the empowerment zone designation as offering new hope that *this* time a poverty neighborhood–centered strategy will really succeed—that *this* package of social services and training programs, on-site housing assistance, and economic development incentives will finally work because it is "comprehensive." The state legislature would avoid biting the bullet on tough, regionwide, fair share housing legislation and tax sharing. City officials would express great confidence in the benefits derived from "community involvement." With considerable fanfare, new social service programs would open neighborhood offices. There would be a few new businesses that, seeking the tax breaks, would have high-profile ribbon-cutting ceremonies in the zone (but most would prove to be uncompetitive and close their doors within a few years). Some high-visibility, non-profit low-income housing projects would be built, but neighborhood groups would successfully block a developer's proposal for the city to acquire and clear a block near the hospital complexes for new condominiums. A few homeowners and landlords would renovate their properties. Some clients of short-term job training programs would secure better jobs (but, with steady paycheck in hand, most would move away). Poverty levels and crime rates would remain high. Attendance and discipline in local public schools would improve, but test scores would remain among the region's lowest. High crime and poor schools would discourage middle class households with children from either remaining or moving into the neighborhood. Five years from now, with the $100 million grubstake in federal cash giving out, *The* Baltimore *Sun* would be running a series of articles on "blasted hopes and shattered dreams" in the empowerment zone. The year 2000 census would report that population was down and poverty up in the target neighborhoods—and that, as a place to live, Baltimore City had continued to fall farther behind its suburbs.

Separate and Unequal

Baltimore City—like almost all inelastic cities—has been down the second path many times before. What is really different this time? Three observations will help to put the empowerment zone program in larger context.

1. The infusion of federal money isn't that much greater than other past and present antipoverty programs. The empowerment zone grant is a one-time infusion of $100 million to be used over a five-year period. The city's current Community Development Block Grant is about $28 million annually from the same federal department (HUD) that is

administering the empowerment zone program. The U.S. Department of Labor provides more than $12 million annually under the Job Training Partnership Act. By 1995 annual federal support for Baltimore City's public housing program reached $206 million (most of which has the effect of chaining the poorest households to the poorest neighborhoods). These programs target a wider geographic area than the three empowerment zone areas, but empowerment zone neighborhoods have always been major participants.

2. The federal government provides equal or greater subsidies and incentives for development outside poverty areas. The empowerment zone grant totals $100 million over five years. By contrast, federal tax policy provides the Baltimore area an estimated $500 million each year to subsidize largely suburban homeowners (through deduction of mortgage interest from federal income tax liability). As another example, Metro Baltimore is allocated $308 million in federal transportation funds for FY 1995. Again, most of the money will flow into suburban-oriented roads and highways.

   To characterize the potential impact of these policies in more human terms, the empowerment zone's population is 72,000, of whom 41 percent are poor. In some target neighborhoods, median household income drops as low as $5,500. One hundred million dollars in empowerment zone grants is about $1,500 per resident over the program's five-year lifetime, or about $300 per year. Out in suburban Howard County, Columbia has 76,000 residents, of whom 3.4 percent are poor. Median household income is $55,000. The estimated tax benefit of mortgage interest deductions for Columbia homeowners also equals about $300 per year per resident.

3. Generating jobs and lifting residents out of poverty make up the empowerment zone's bottom line. Stimulated by the $100 million in federal funds and $225 million in tax credits, planners project creation of 8,895 new jobs over a ten-year period. That is about the same number of jobs as are created in suburban Baltimore every six months. For $325 million, the federal government could pay five years' rent for standard apartments, scattered throughout suburban Baltimore, for over 9,000 poor households. Such an effort would not only allow all poor households to move

from the empowerment zone, but also place them in an environment that is experiencing *20 times the rate of new job creation.*

This last observation is not an argument for total evacuation of the empowerment zone but is made to underscore the fact that *as the arena of social and economic opportunity, the real "empowerment zone" is the whole metropolitan area—the city and its suburbs.*

This is a lesson that the U.S. government has generally refused to acknowledge because it is politically uncomfortable. So the federal government has launched one program after another targeting inner-city neighborhoods. Whether the prescription has been the infusion of tax dollars (the Big Buck strategy), the infusion of economic and moral incentives (the Big Bootstrap strategy), or both together (the empowerment zones), the basic philosophy is the same: Quarantine "them" in inner-city ghettos and barrios away from "us" and help "them" build from within—with money or suasion. Both ideological camps believe that separate can be made equal, or at least equal enough to be tolerable.

"Separate but equal" cannot work. It has never worked. But our fears inhibit most citizens and most elected officials from bridging the chasm and no longer relying on such strategies. So doomed inner-city programs keep being touted—with, in my view, the Clinton Administration's empowerment zones as the latest wrapping on an old package.

TRANSFORMING PUBLIC HOUSING

Three days before the much ballyhooed announcement of the designated empowerment zone communities, HUD Secretary Henry Cisneros announced another series of proposals, packaged as HUD's "Reinvention Blueprint." One of the three main goals of the Secretary's proposals is gaining Congressional approval to "totally transform HUD's public housing programs over the next three years."

"Public housing projects," Cisneros noted, "have become traps for the poorest of the poor rather than a launching pad for families trying to improve their lives. In some communities public housing has worked, but in many others tens of thousands of people—mostly women and children—are living in squalid conditions at a very high cost of wasted lives and federal dollars."

Cisneros described the primary goals as follows:

- We would give public housing residents a *genuine market choice*—to stay where they are or move to apartments in the private rental

market. Operating and capital subsidies for local housing authorities would be converted to Housing Certificates for Families and
Individuals.

- We would *break the monopoly* of local housing authorities over federal housing resources. We would require housing authorities to
compete in the marketplace with private landlords to attract
renters with Housing Certificates.

- In the Housing Certificate program we will give preference to
families that are moving toward self-sufficiency by already working or participating in "work-ready" and education programs.

- We will end the blight in distressed inner-city neighborhoods
caused by many public housing projects by accelerating the de-
molition of uninhabitable and non-viable properties. We will not
support new developments that are exclusively occupied by the
very poor.

Over a three-year transition, HUD would convert all project-
based public housing subsidies to tenant-based rental assistance.
During FY 1996 and FY 1997, HUD would deregulate more than
3,000 well-performing local authorities, work to reform more than
100 severely troubled authorities, and divest 10–15 of the most
troubled local authorities that are beyond any reasonable hope of
improvement of their properties and management control. During
FY 1996, HUD would consolidate all public housing funds into a
Capital Fund and Operating Subsidies Fund. States and localities
could opt to receive all housing funds as Housing Certificates. By
FY 1998, all former project-based public housing subsidies would
be completely portable Housing Certificates awarded to eligible
low-income households.

The philosophy of Cisneros' plan should appeal to the new Republican Congressional majority. The politics of Cisneros' plan
probably will not. However, regardless of the plan's short-term
fate, the longer trend is to close large public housing projects,
which have become major tools of economic and racial segregation
in urban America.

Any reasonable success of Cisneros' proposals will have far
more impact on reducing racial and economic isolation and opening up opportunity for Baltimore City's poorest residents than the
empowerment zone. In 1994, the Housing Authority of Baltimore
City owned and operated 15,983 low-income housing units—over
80 percent were grouped in projects ranging from the 20-unit
Spencer Gardens to the giant, 949-unit Hollander Ridge. By contrast, the housing authority was allocated only 6,289 certificates
and vouchers to subsidize rents of low-income families in private
rental housing. Only 1,000 of these certificates and vouchers were

"portable"—that is, they could be used to rent housing outside the city limits; slightly over half of the recipients had moved into Baltimore County. For FY 1995, the Housing Authority's annual operating budget was almost $206 million—twice the total one-time federal cash infusion for the empowerment zone.

It is hard to overstate the contribution Baltimore City's public housing program has made to ghettoizing poor blacks. Over 90 percent of all public housing residents are black. Aside from units for the elderly (about 13 percent of the total), over 90 percent of the tenant households are headed by single mothers. As was discussed in Chapter Three, there are 31 city census tracts where the poverty rate exceeds 40 percent. There is a large public housing project located in or next to every one of those census tracts.

In Baltimore City—as in many communities—public housing offers shelter for many but opportunity for few. In Secretary Cisneros' words, HUD's housing assistance programs must become "platforms of opportunity" for poor households. HUD has finally recognized what works. Integration works.

Does moving poor households out of economic ghettos into better communities reduce levels of unemployment, welfare dependency, school dropouts, crime and delinquency, drug addiction and alcoholism associated with a high concentration of such households in their former neighborhoods?

The answer is "yes." Helping poor people leave bad neighborhoods is the most effective antipoverty program. Good housing mobility programs are the most effective ways to improve school achievement and employment opportunities for poor families. In the postindustrial Information Age, education is the key that unlocks the door to adult success more than ever. The quickest path to securing high-quality education for a child from a poor household is to place the child in an already good school. High-performing neighborhood schools are almost invariably located in predominantly middle class neighborhoods, which are now generally concentrated in the suburbs.

There are many studies on how poverty affects educational performance. I myself have studied the test performance of 1,108 children from public housing households who attended the Albuquerque Public Schools from 1982 to 1992. The study found that the socioeconomic level of a public housing child's classmates and their level of academic performance are important influences on the public housing child's own performance. The study found that the difference between a public housing child's living in a poor neighborhood and attending a neighborhood school where 80 percent of his or her classmates are also poor and that child's living in a middle class neighborhood and attending that neighborhood school where 20 percent of the children are poor is a 13 percentile improvement in the child's test scores!

As city-based factory jobs shrink, the bulk of new retail and service industry jobs are being created in suburbs. Residents of inner-city neighborhoods may face significant transportation barriers to reaching new suburban employment locations. Even if transportation is available, traveling long distances may be too expensive or unfeasible to justify taking lower-skilled, lower-wage jobs at suburban locations. Living nearer to the job can cut back commuting costs significantly.

One of the more carefully studied examples of the effects of moving poor families from inner-city ghettos to suburbs is the Chicago area's Gautreaux Assisted Housing Project (already discussed on page 81). Under federal court order, since 1976, the Chicago Housing Authority has provided 5,600 Section 8 rent vouchers to allow eligible pubic housing households to move out of CHA's notorious high-rise projects into privately owned rental housing. As of mid-1994, approximately 3,000 Gautreaux households have moved to 115 of Chicago's 232 suburbs, the great majority into Northwest Cook County, an area of upper middle income housing and rapid job growth. Another 2,600 Gautreaux households have elected to rent private apartments within Chicago itself. Virtually all participants are black households headed by single mothers with two or three children. On entering the program, almost all were receiving welfare payments; 44 percent were second-generation welfare recipients.

Researchers have compared the outcomes for "suburban-movers" versus "city-movers." Of the suburban-movers, 64 percent were working compared with 51 percent for city-mover mothers. Of the suburban-mover children, 95 percent graduated from their suburban school systems compared with a graduation rate of 80 percent from Chicago schools. Fifty-four percent of suburban movers had continued their education (27 percent in four-year colleges) compared with 21 percent of the city-movers (4 percent in four-year colleges). Seven-five percent of suburban-mover youths were working (21 percent for hourly wages of $6.50 or better); by contrast, 41 percent of city-mover youths had jobs (5 percent for $6.50 an hour or better). Though not studied, educational and employment outcomes for both suburban-movers and city-movers were presumably much better than for those who stayed in Chicago's South Side public housing ghetto. The study concluded that the program revealed that *these low-income people had capabilities that were not evident when they lived in the city.* Adults were able to get jobs and youth were able to do much better in school, but these capabilities were hidden in the city. . . . Situational factors can suppress achievement below one's abilities. The suburban move seems to have removed these suppressing influences on achievement, and much higher education and job achievements emerged. But these capabilities did not emerge in similar people who moved to city neighborhoods. Rather, some features of the suburbs seemed to allow or encourage these capabilities to emerge.

As one participant in the Gautreaux Project summed up her experience: "A housing project deteriorates you. You don't want to do anything. Living in the suburbs made me feel that I'm worth something. I can do anything I want to do if I get up and try it."

High crime rates are also the product of high concentration of poverty. Crime moves upward with a neighborhood's rate of poverty, but at neighborhood poverty rate levels above 15 to 20 percent, the crime rate increases faster than the poverty rate. When a neighborhood moves back down the poverty curve by decreasing the concentration of poverty, crime rates fall faster than the poverty rate.

Middle class Americans really should not be skeptical about the negative influence of bad neighborhoods on poor residents. Middle class Americans place the highest value on the impact of good communities on their own lives. When buying a home, most middle class families do not make the decision fundamentally on the basis of the quality of the *shelter* they are purchasing. They are making a judgment about the quality of the *community* that they are joining. How safe is the neighborhood? How good are the schools? Are the new neighbors *people like us* (an important factor for some, at least)? There is little doubt about the importance attributed to a good community environment by middle class Americans.

Why, then, is there such widespread unwillingness to credit the negative impact of poverty neighborhoods for a substantial amount of the crime, delinquency, and welfare dependency that are endemic in poor neighborhoods? In part, the answer lies in another element of our value system: the concept of individual responsibility. *Those people don't have jobs . . . are on welfare . . . have too many babies . . . are drug addicts . . . commit crimes because they aren't acting responsibly. If they would only act like us, they could advance in the world just as we have.* The notion that poor people are caught up in a self-created "culture of poverty" has gained a growing audience in recent years.

Society cannot abandon the principle that individuals must be responsible for their own actions. It is, indeed, a glue that holds a civilized society together far better than rewards and sanctions. In fact, however, there are large numbers of poor people who are eager to take such responsibility by moving themselves and their families out of poverty-impacted neighborhoods into better communities. They have heretofore been denied the opportunity.

The skepticism about the positive impact of better environments on poor people's behavior is really based on fear. And that fear is used to justify erecting barriers to try to keep *them* away from *us*.

More than anything else, it is that fear—fear of the explosive mixture of poverty and race—that prevents the Baltimore area from doing what must be done to dissolve the social dynamite that grows in inner-city ghettos. The public furor whipped up in eastern Baltimore County during the spring of 1994 was a sad example of such fears. HUD had selected the Baltimore area as one of five metro areas to participate in its "Moving To Opportunity" program. Some 150 special Section 8 rent vouchers were provided to allow public housing households to move from Baltimore City housing projects specifically into suburban rental housing. Suburban neighborhoods that already had higher levels of poverty (i.e., above 10 percent poverty) were placed off limits for use of the rent vouchers. Coordinating arrangements had been quietly made between city and county housing officials.

In the context of the year's political campaigns, however, the program was a tempting target for demagoguery. Several candidates for county office began to pound the drums, sounding tribal alarms. Right-wing talk show hosts jumped aboard. Angry protest meetings were organized in Essex and Dundalk in eastern Baltimore County. HUD, city and county officials, and a local nonprofit agency involved came under public siege. Finally, Maryland's U.S. Senators, alarmed during an election year, stepped in and canceled the second year's appropriation for the entire national program.

One can sympathize with the residents of Essex, for example. Over the past two decades, they have seen the number of poor residents—black and white—more than double in their community. Some long-term residents—blue collar families—have been thrown on hard times by vanishing factory jobs. Others are newcomers moving into the community, attracted by its low-cost housing supply. Surrounded by rising crime rates, feeling a sense of community deterioration, and being anxious about conserving the value of their homes (a lifetime's equity), many Essex residents were easy targets for emotional propaganda against the Moving To Opportunity program, despite the fact that most Essex neighborhoods would have been exempted from participation.

In fact, it is precisely older, inner suburbs like Dundalk and Essex that, next to Baltimore City itself, will benefit most from the housing policies recommended in the previous chapter. Without strong policies and programs promoting mixed-income development *throughout the entire Baltimore area,* the decline of many hand-me-down neighborhoods in older, inner suburbs is as inevitable as the continued ghettoization of inner-city Baltimore. Targeting "fair share" low- and moderate-income housing on new construction, primarily in the outlying counties, will relieve the adverse market pressures on older suburbs. Many Dundalk and Essex neighborhoods already have more than their fair share of the metro area's poor households. If they are to be stabilized, they desperately need the very policies and programs I have recommended.

The Baltimore area is hardly alone in its fears. Fear is crippling many of America's urban areas. Fear blinds too many people from seeing what the core of the problem is—racial and class segregation. And fear immobilizes too many from seeing strategies that really work, such as mixed-income communities in which poor people—a relatively small proportion of most metropolitan communities—are integrated into mainstream society, its standards, and its opportunities. The fact that so few communities aggressively pursue policies like Montgomery County's MPDU/HOC programs is more a measure of the extent of the fear than rawest ignorance of what should be done.

Thirty years ago, a Labor Department colleague once defined a federal "demonstration program" as "what we do when we don't want to spend the money to solve the problem." But it really is not even money that is the barrier to action. Certainly solutions to society's deepest problems cost money. This report has not offered any recommendations that are free.

But America's wealth is immense. Compared to the scale of its toughest social problem, the Baltimore region's own wealth is fully adequate. The policies I've suggested for the Metro Tax Base Pool would mean less than a 5 percent increase in areawide property tax payments. Property taxes are about half of all local revenues raised by county governments, and in Maryland, locally raised county revenues (including public school funds) average about 6 percent of personal income. Thus, *the small property tax increase proposed would actually represent an increase of about two-tenths of 1 percent of personal income.*

For that monetary sacrifice, the Baltimore region could substantially end the high concentration of poor people in Baltimore City neighborhoods and arrest the spread of poverty into older suburbs of Baltimore County and Anne Arundel County. The key is to have the right policy and to apply that policy in a sustained, consistent manner over 15–20 years. Of all the strategies I've studied, mixed-income housing strategies are easily the most effective—and the best has been carried out right next door to Baltimore in Montgomery County.

Montgomery County's 20-year experience demonstrates another truth: It is often far more difficult to contemplate adopting such policies than actually to carry them out. The thought is more intimidating than the deed.

What the Baltimore region needs is a political breakthrough. In light of other states' experience, that breakthrough must come from the Maryland General Assembly and the governor of Maryland. The policies recommended are neither politically painless nor politically easy. Poverty and race are the toughest political issues in America. It will require the vision, the will, and political courage from state legislators and the governor to put Maryland's signature city back on the path of renewal.

This task cannot be accomplished without strong citizen support. Legislators and governors do not require a clear majority of the public applauding their positions to address the state's more controversial problems. But they need *some* public supporters calling for action.

It is, however, incumbent on Maryland's political leaders to act now, for there is traditionally another forum for achieving major social policy changes: the federal and state courts. Segregation by race has been against the law of the land since the U.S. Supreme Court's epochal *Brown* v. *Board of Education* ruling in 1954. There is a growing body of litigation seeking to establish that systems of governance that lead to wide fiscal, social, and economic disparities among local jurisdictions are denials of the constitutional right to equal protection of the laws for poor minority city residents. Connecticut's *Scheff* v. *O'Neill* is merely the most prominent of such cases.

In my view, reform achieved through the political process is preferable to reform ordered by the courts. The recommendations offered for action in this report are undoubtedly not the perfect solution for the Baltimore region's problems. In all the case studies presented in Chapter One, the political process made changes in the original recommendations put forth by reform advocates—and these changes were almost always for the good.

I've proposed that the Maryland General Assembly establish a Metropolitan Municipality of Greater Baltimore, governed by a popularly elected Metro Council and Metro Executive, empowered to carry out regionwide low- and moderate-income housing strategies, and financed principally by a broad-based Metro Tax Base Pool with modest impact on the average citizen's tax bill. The recommendations have several advantages:

- All recommendations are based on successful models in other communities (Portland, Toronto, Minneapolis–St. Paul, Montgomery County, etc.).
- Metro would fill the policy gap that local governments find impossible to fill through voluntary agreements but would still leave local governments in place to deliver general services efficiently to their citizens.
- Metro would be a flexible instrument for unified metropolitan action; it could expand geographically as future development trends justify, and, beyond its core planning and housing mission, it could expand the scope of its policies and programs as directed by the legislature, local governments, or local citizens by popular referendum.
- Metro's vital housing role would be financed directly out of the Metro Tax Base Pool through a modest tax increase that represents only two-tenths of 1 percent of personal income of its constituents. Though coordinating existing federal- and state-funded activities would be important, achieving the region's low-income housing goals would not depend financially on tax support external to the Baltimore area.
- Metro would be directly accountable to the citizens of metro Baltimore through election of its chief executive and governing body. And while its task would be to confront the metro area's toughest issue, it would do so through forging a greater consciousness of metropolitan *community*.

Baltimore City has many strengths and assets. Its downtown business district, universities, and hospitals continue to be major regional centers of high-quality employment. It has a legacy of wonderful urban neighborhoods; our ancestors knew how to create urban environments of convenience, diversity, and charm. However, Baltimore's physical geography is now overwhelmed by its unbalanced human geography—a geography in which insurmountable social barriers are thrown up by the powerful forces unleashed by the concentration of poverty. Many middle class people would prefer to live nearer city-based jobs. Middle class households would repopulate interesting urban neighborhoods if they could be assured of reasonable safety and good schools. City neighborhoods that were once strong, middle class communities can become so again if some sociological breathing space can be opened up.

Of course, nobody needs safer neighborhoods and better schools more than the current residents of poverty-impacted neighborhoods do. For many, however, the surest path to safer neighborhoods and better schools is to leave inner-city ghettos for better opportunities that are already in place elsewhere in the metro area.

"Diversity, balance, stability"—these must be the watchwords for both diversifying the suburbs and restoring Baltimore City.

Metro Baltimore stands at the threshold of the 21st century. The State of Maryland must summon the political will and the political courage to regain for the Baltimore region the front rank among American communities it once proudly held. City and suburb—we are all in it together.

LIST OF SOURCES

All data not otherwise indicated are taken from publications of the Bureau of the Census of the U.S. Department of Commerce, covering the decennial censuses from 1950 to 1990, or from studies, conducted by the author, based on official census data.

CHAPTER ONE

The observations on municipal bond ratings are based on analysis of *Moody's State and Local Government Data Book (1991)*, updated by information supplied the author by The Bond Buyer in November 1993.

The calculations of residential segregation rates in Table 1.7 are drawn from Roderick J. Harrison and Daniel H. Weinberg, "Racial and Ethnic Segregation in 1990," U.S. Bureau of the Census, Washington, D.C., April 1992. Similar calculations on school segregation have been made by Maris Mikelsons of The Urban Institute and the author. The data source is a special tape prepared for the author by the National Center for Education Statistics of the U.S. Department of Education.

All information on metro area employment trends from 1973 to 1988 in Tables 1.10–1.12 comes from *Regional Projections to 2040: Volume 2, Metropolitan Statistical Areas*, published by the U.S. Commerce Department's Bureau of Economic Analysis (October 1990). Information for employment in 1950 is derived from the 1950 census.

The metropolitan cost-of-living adjustments on which Tables 1.13, 1.14, and 1.15 are based have been developed by the author, using median single-family home values and median monthly contract rent tabulations from the 1950 and 1990 censuses. The relative cost-of-housing indices derived are then combined with indices for the costs of food, clothing, health care, and transportation from Richard Boyer and David Savageau, *Places Rated Almanac*, Simon & Schuster, New York (1989).

154

CHAPTER TWO

The analysis of state laws regarding annexation and city-county consolidation in Tables 2.3 and 2.4 are adapted from U.S. Advisory Commission on Intergovernmental Relations, *State Laws Governing Local Government Structure and Administration*, Washington, D.C., Government Printing Office (March 1993).

The discussion of the administrative organization and governmental powers of the three consolidated city-county governments has been adapted (with minimal paraphrasing) from a consultant report prepared for the Wyandotte County Commission to Study Consolidation (James L. Kenworthy, *Local Government Reorganization in Wyandotte County, Kansas*, Washington, D.C., and Kansas City, MO, Scott Gard Associates (March 1988).

Historical information on Jacksonville is drawn from Richard Martin, *A Quiet Revolution: The Consolidation of Jacksonville–Duval County and the Dynamics of Urban Political Reform*, White Publishing Company, Jacksonville, FL (1993) and *Consolidated Jacksonville: Twenty-Five Years of Progress*, published by the Consolidation Commemorative Committee of the Jacksonville Chamber of Commerce (October 1, 1993). The quotation on page 39 is from *Consolidated Jacksonville*. Mayor Austin and Mayor Tanzler's comments were made in the author's presence.

A fascinating history of the creation of Unigov is found in C. James Owen and York Willbern, *Governing Metropolitan Indianapolis: The Politics of Unigov*, University of California Press, Berkeley, CA (1985). The quotations on page 43, including those from *The Wall Street Journal* article, are found on pages 196–197 of that book.

These readings are supplemented by field visits and discussions the author has had with principals in both of these communities.

The history of the consolidation of King County, Washington, and Metro is based on "King County-Metro: A New Government," a report written by David Gering and issued by the King County Council in July 1993 and supplemented by field visits and discussions.

The assessment of voluntary councils of government is quoted from "Regional Civic Governance: Emerging Organizational Structure and Strategies: A Proposal of the National Civic League (August 1991).

A report entitled "Historical Development of the Metropolitan Service District," prepared for the Metro Home Rule Charter Committee by Carl and Margery Post Abbott (May 1991) is the basic source for the history of the evolution of Portland Metro plus the author's conversations with Metro staff.

The list of governmental powers and other material regarding Metro Toronto are adapted from Albert Rose, *Governing Metropolitan Toronto: A Social and Political Analysis, 1953–1971,* University of California Press, Berkeley, CA (1972). Also very helpful is a chapter by Frances Frisken, "Planning and Servicing the Greater Toronto Area: The Interplay of Provincial and Municipal Interests," in Donald R. Rosenblatt and Andrew Sancton, eds., *Metropolitan Governance: American/Canadian Perspectives,* University of California Press, Berkeley, CA (1993). Frederick Gardiner's valedictory remarks are quoted on page 165 of Professor Rose's book. Professor Frisken provides the judgments quoted on page 58.

The basic source on Connecticut's Affordable Housing Appeals Process, including the quotation on page 61, is Melinda Westbrook, "Connecticut's New Affordable Housing Appeals Procedure Assaulting the Presumptive Validity of Land Use Decisions," *Connecticut Bar Journal* (June 1992). The quotations regarding the recommendations of the Regionalism Collaborative Process come from the report of the chair to the Connecticut legislative leadership in February 1994. The author has done extensive work in Connecticut during the last three years.

Information on Montgomery County's housing programs comes from a booklet entitled "HOC Housing Programs: The Work of the Housing Opportunities Commission of Montgomery County, Maryland" (June 1992); Monica Shah, "An Explanation and Examination of the Moderately-Priced Dwelling Unit Program in Montgomery County, Maryland," a paper prepared for the Housing Law Seminar of the Georgetown University Law Center (July 19, 1993); and information provided by the author by HOC staff. The resale price study cited is "A Comparison of the Appreciation Rate of Homes in Montgomery County Communities with and without Moderately-Priced Dwelling Units (MPDUs)" prepared by William L. Berry & Co., Inc. (December 1988). Additional information comes from the author's discussions with Bernard Tetrault, the HOC's director, and Richard Tustian, former county planner.

All data regarding the Twin Cities Fiscal Disparities Plan is taken from "Tax-Base sharing in the Twin Cities Metropolitan Area: Taxes payable in 1995" prepared for the Metropolitan Council (February 1995). This is supplemented by extensive visits and discussions the author has had in the Twin Cities area.

The housing studies of Professor Tom Bier and his colleagues are summarized in a document from The Ohio University Program. Cleveland State University (June 27, 1990).

CHAPTER THREE

Data on Baltimore City's revenue structure and regional property tax rates are taken from an unpublished report by Marsha Schachtel entitled "The Paradox of Baltimore City: Healthy Economy, Empty Pockets," prepared for the Abell Foundation in 1992.

The op-ed article by Theo Lippman appeared in the Baltimore *Sun* on November 15, 1993.

Information on the history of Richmond's annexation controversies comes from John V. Moeser and Rutledge M. Dennis, *The Politics of Annexation: Oligarchic Power in A Southern City*, Schenkman Publishing Company, Cambridge, MA (1982).

The discussion of the tax base trends for the Baltimore region is derived from information in the *Census of Government, Vol. 2: Government Finances*, which the Census Bureau compiles every five years. The first reports of the 1992 Census of Governments were released as this book was in page proofs. Since Tables 3.17–3.24 are intended to be illustrative rather than definitive, we chose to use data from 1966–1986 (i.e., from the quinennial censuses, beginning in 1967 through 1987) to ensure comparability of data. The Census of Governments does not provide data for Queen Anne's County for the earliest years. Therefore, Queen Anne's County was excluded from the tables; however, it would be covered by the Metro Tax Base Pool.

CONCLUSION

Information on Baltimore City's empowerment zone is drawn from a document entitled "Baltimore Empowerment Strategic Plan" and articles published in the Baltimore *Sun* on December 22, 1994.

The author's study cited is "The Academic Performance of Public Housing Children: Does Living in Middle Class Neighborhoods and Attending Middle Class Schools Make a Difference?" with Jeffrey Mosley, The Urban Institute Press, Washington D.C., (unpublished).

The classic evaluation of the Gautreaux Program is James E. Rosenbaum et al., "Black Pioneers—Do Their Moves to the Suburbs Increase Economic Opportunity for Mothers and Children?" in *Federal National Mortgage Association (Fannie Mae), Housing Policy Debate*, Vol. 2.4, pp. 1179–1213.

The study of crime in Minneapolis cited is Myron Orfield and Steven Cannon, "The Effect of Concentrated Poverty on Crime: A Case Study of Minneapolis, MN," (unpublished).

INDEX